All Middos

Rabbi Jonathan Rietti

All Middos Begin with a Thought
by Rabbi Jonathan Rietti

Copyright © 2019 Rabbi Jonathan Rietti

All rights reserved. No part of this publication may be reproduced, distributed, or transmitted in any form or by any means, including photocopying, recording, or other electronic or mechanical methods, without the prior written permission of the publisher, except in the case of brief quotations embodied in critical reviews and certain other noncommercial uses permitted by copyright law. For permission requests, write to the publisher, addressed "Attention: Permissions Coordinator," at the address below.

office@breakthroughchinuch.com

ISBN 9781703465372
10 9 8 7 6 5 4 3 2 1
1. Religion 2. Education

First Edition

Printed in the United States of America

Table of Contents

	Introduction to Middos	1
1.1	Giving Context to Middos. Hashkafa behind Middos	3
1.2	When do Children Begin Learning Middos?	8
2.0	Will The Real You Please Stand Up? You Are Tzelem Elokim	9
2.1	Define Middos	10
2.2	Can Middos be taught or only learned?	12
2.3	Identify the one core mechanic that regulates our Middos	12
2.4	The True Mind-Emotion Relationship in One Word - Lev	13
2.5	Defining Lev as Mind	14
2.6	Hilchos Middos is really Halachos of the mind! Reality-Thinking Vs. Non-Reality-Thinking..	17
2.7	Middos in Taryag Mitzvos	18
2.8	Middos not listed in Taryag Mitzvos (Miderabanan)	26
3.0	The Mitzvah of Tochacha	29
3.1	How Does Hashem want me to respond to hardships in life?	29
3.2	Plan A - The Mitzvah Not to Think - But Thank Instead!	30
3.3	Plan B- Judging others is not my business!	32
3.4	Plan C. Give Tochacha. Here are the Rules - Hilchos Tochacha	33

Practical Applications for learning Middos through role modeling scenarios.

3.5	The Tochacha Formula - 3 Steps! That's all!	35
3.6	Dear Rebbe/Morah, Who Are you and Who Are You not?	35
	In My Role as 'Rebbe/Morah' Am I also Policeman, Judge, or Arbitrator?	
3.7	Sample Scenario - Role Model Tochacha	36
3.8	Examples of Tochacha - Using Puppets	43
4.0	Metaphors to understand How My Middos come from Thought	44
4.1	#1 - The Music of your Innate Health, Neshama, is always playing	44
4.2	#2 - What options do you have when a pop up shows on your phone?	47
4.3	#3 - Your Mind is Your Garden - Don't Water the Weeds!	51
4.4	#4 - What's The Tiny Black Dot in the Middle!	53
4.5	#5 - Is the Spider Real or Fake?	57
4.6	#6 - How Much is This Bill Worth?	58
4.7	#7 - Ten Pin Bowling	64
4.8	#8 - A Rolls Royce Vs a 67 Chevy	66
4.9	#9 - Think It Over, But Don't Over-Think It! The Real Problem is Over-Weight Thinking!	67
4.10	#10 - My Mind is My Palace! Select your own paintings & furnishings!	69
4.11	#11 - The WWWW.Con (The World Wide Web of Waste.CON)	73
4.12	#12 - Thoughts Going Around Inside Me & The Airport Carousel	76
4.13	#13 - Why Would Anyone Repeatedly Beat *Themselves* Up?	79
4.14	#14 - Why carry a sack of other people's hammers to hit yourself?	83
4.15	#15 - Carrying a sack of painful memories wherever I go!	86
4.16	#16 - Returning one's hand to the burning stove!	87
4.17	#17 - Your Internal Windshield Wipers	89
4.18	#18 - Man with Pneumonia keeps sneezing and coughing in other people's faces!	91
4.19	#19 - Select your own weather! You were born with your own internal Weather System!	92
4.20	#20 - "I'll Do It My Waze!" You come with your own GPS system!	94
4.21	#21 - Phew! It was only a dream! The Nightmare Metaphor	95
4.22	#22 - The Sun is Always Shining! True or False?	96
4.23	#23 - Imagine Your car has two steering wheels!	97
4.24	#24 - The Horse & Rider Metaphor - Who is taking who for a ride?	98
4.25	#25 - Rain drops leaking through the roof and flooding your home!	99
4.26	#26 - The King Hired His General to Stir a Rebellion!	102
4.27	#27 - Latest Touch Screen Technology - Mind-Emotion-Touch-Screen	106
4.28	#28 - How High-Tech Advertising is a Metaphor for how Hashem runs the world!	109
5.0	Stories of Tzadikim to Inspire Middos Tovos	116
6.0	The Art of the Sale. The Mechanics of Teaching Middos	117

Introduction:

The Goal of This Booklet
The goal of this booklet is to inspire adults to help children give birth to their own innate resilience.

The premise is that children are born with innate resilience. To put it more directly, we are all born with resilience as part of our Divine DNA. Our job, as parents and teachers is to help our children give birth to the Divinely injected resilience already inside them.[1]

Beside whatever children inherit of their parent's genes, we are all created בצלם אלקים a 'reflection of Elokim.' This means 'unlimited in your power to emulate Hashem.'[2] The חלק אלוקה inside you, driving you, is what gives you the power to think. You have that power at your fingertips at all times because you are always only one thought away from your next thought. Always one thought away from changing your mind.[3]

This premise, that we all have innate resilience has huge implications. If we can help children actually experience their own innate resilience, they will have access to the master key to open the doors to all Middos Tovos and the very same master key that closes the doors from letting Middos Raos enter the mind!

This book will show you how Tikkun HaMiddos is inherently the very purpose of all creation. Teaching ourselves to self-correct is a gift we all have all the time. Every element in creation has the Divine Intelligence to self-heal because we are all made of the same creation-material, Hashem's Intelligence.

The Structure of This Book
The structure of this book is divided into two parts. Firstly, the essential Hashkafa behind Middos and secondly, the practical applications of how to help children teach themselves Middos. We

---

1 See Metzudas David on Mishley 23:24-25 where he shows the word מלמד as coming from the root יולד - giving birth. He then defines a Melamed as one who causes the birth of wisdom in the mind of the student! The function of the teacher/Melamed is less about teaching information than it has to do with help the child discover they can find the answers inside themselves! See also the Gra on Avot. 5:3 where he claims the power of Avraham Avinu to stand up to all ten trials is now part of Zera Avraham too. So, in essence, we all have Avraham Avinu's innate ability to stand up to our trials. That is why, explains the Gra, the Mishna calls him Avraham Avinu. Avinu, our father because we inherited his power to stand up to life's nisyonos.

2 See Gen. 1:26 and Seforno. See Sefer HaChinuch, Mitzvah #39 where he defines man as his mind, שכל powered by the Neshama.

3 The very term תשובה הרהור really means a 'change in thought' or 'redirected thought.'

encourage you to read the entire Hashkafa sections from 1.1 till 2.8 because it really helps you experience for yourself how all Middos are born in the thought of the moment, from moment to moment. Then you will have a deeper appreciation of the power of the 28 Metaphors to help children experience their own ability to change what they are thinking. They will be able to pull themselves out from the trap of people and circumstances dictating their thoughts and emotions, to recognizing that nobody or anything has the power to make me think or feel anything I don't want to think. It is in this experience children will discover their innate resilience is always with them to call upon to align them to Tikkun HaMiddos.

Our Tefila is that this booklet help parents and teachers help children reveal their Tzelem Elokim in all it shinning resilience so that they will remain strong in their love for Hashem and His Torah at the greeting of Mashiach Tzidkeinu, may he come soon in our days, Amen.

1.1 Giving Context to Middos

What if we are all created with inner resilience?
What if our innate resilience is only one thought away?
What if Hashem gave us all the same power to tap into our next thought?
What if all Middos are actually thought in the moment?
What if we are all only one thought away from changing a Midda?
What if Jealousy is really a thought in the moment?
What if Anger is really thought in the moment?
What if Anxiety is actually a thought-induced state?
What if Happiness is really a thought?
What if it is true that the life of a thought is only as long as I think it?
If the life of a thought is only as long as I think it, then how far away am I from the next thought?
I am always one thought away! Always!
What if it is true that in one moment of thought, a person can elect to be a Tzadik in Hashem's dictionary?[4]
What if unhappiness is an innocent misunderstanding of reality?
What if worry and anxiety are misunderstandings of reality?
What if Hashem already gave us instructions about how to think? How to change faulty thinking, and made it available to anyone, any time in any circumstance?

If all or any of the above is true, then our lives would begin a whole new journey of discovery. Discovery of the inside out approach to life! Inside out means the Mitzvos of the Mind would guide me to let go of the ill-logic of thinking other people or circumstances are controlling my emotions. That is never true. The moment I surrender to blaming anyone or anything, I have also said they control my life and I cannot control my life! But that is never true, nothing controls my life, but my own thought in the moment.

Hashem is Perfect and everything He created is perfect. In His perfect world, nothing is wasted.

Billions of people have been born in the almost 6,000 since creation of Adam. They all died, where are they? Billions of animals, birds and insects have died, where are they all?
They were buried in the soil, decomposed and gave back to the earth they came from!

---

[4] Shulchan Aruch, Even HaEzer, 38:31.

Trillions of fish have died in the oceans over the past thousands of years, where are they all?
Decomposed or eaten by other fish and thus provided life giving nourishment to the oceans, because that is part of Hashem's perfect design.

Rain falls from the skies into the ground, where does it go?
Underground rivers form where the water hits solid rock and trickles out through the top soil to form springs, streams and rivers.

The water in the top soil is retained by the grass and roots of trees and plant life which is purposely designed to absorb the moisture in the soil through its roots up into its stem and then grow into branches and leaves to absorb sunlight and turn it into life giving oxygen! Nothing is wasted. All is good and all elements in creation obey Hashem's every detailed command in their mission to provide the perfect conditions for MAN to Live on earth.

How does this all happen?

Every rain drop has Divine Intelligence,
Every seed is guided by Divine Intelligence,
Every root, stem, trunk, branch, leaf is guided by Diving Intelligence.

Your body began as a putrid drop, at the time of conception, your brain and heart were literally microscopic, yet, over the next 40 days you created your own
- Skeletal system,
- Muscular system,
- Respiratory system,
- Nervous system,
- Lymph system.
- Your skin, your muscles, your sinews, limbs - you literally created yourself !!

How is this possible?
Only because of Divine Intelligence imbued in you, your Neshama no less, created your entire body.

Everything you are in the physical world is made from Divine Intelligence.
Everything you experience in the physical world is made of Divine Intelligence.

The destruction from volcanic lava is actually the rebirth of that very soil burned by the lava.
The destruction of entire forests from fire is actually the rebirth of its soil which regrows millions of tress from the fertilizing ashes!

Not only is there no waste, if there is ever a wound inflicted on planet earth, it is actually part of the planets very maintenance!

Every element in creation has Divine Intelligence to create itself and to heal itself! Self-Correct!

If one has a cut on the skin, or a broken bone. The body knows exactly what to do to regenerate the cells which will heal the broken bone and give you new skin!

Is it conceivable that the same Divine Intelligence which gives creative and self-healing power, *would not have the same power to heal the mind*?!

Your mind was the purpose of all creation! Hashem did not create the universe, galaxies and stars for the sake of the galaxies and stars.

Hashem did not create all of planet earth with its land forms, oceans, mountains, valleys and rivers for themselves.

Hashem did not create all the plant and animal kingdoms for themselves.

Hashem created all of creation for Mankind!

But not for the body of man!

The body was created for your mind, for you to exercise free will with every next thought!

Would Hashem give all elements in creation the Divine Intelligence to know how to heal themselves, except the mind!

That is inconceivable!

Your mind is never broken.

You are never scarred by painful memories!

You are never damaged because of trauma from the past!

Every human being is sitting in the middle of mental health, they just may not be aware of it!

No person, no matter how much they have suffered or have been traumatized is relegated to a second class experience of life. This is impossible. Because Hashem gave each of us the power of......the next thought.

Babies are born happy!

Happiness is already inside you.[5]

You are never broken.

Even if you have been traumatized or pained in the past, that is now only a memory, nothing more! A past memory does not exist because reality does not exist in the past, reality exists only in your thought - NOW.

The past is dead history! The future never exists because as soon as you arrive there it is the present. So you actually only live one day, one hour, one moment at a time, moment to moment. Should I spend that moment thinking about pain and trauma?

In one moment of thought, a person can elect to be a Tzadik in Hashem's dictionary!

Bechira is the true purpose of all creation![6]

The ultimate freedom of choice, *is knowing -*
You can think anything you want,
Anytime,
In any circumstance,
In any place.

---

5   Tehilim 4:8 - נָתַתָּה שִׂמְחָה בְלִבִּי - Literally - "You have gifted Happiness in my mind." The verse is in past tense, so David HaMelech is describing something already given to him, he already has in his mind, all the reasons to be happy! Happiness is the natural default. Happiness is Logic-All, All-Logic. Unhappiness is Ill-Logic, unhealthy thinking!

6   See Sichos HaRan #300. If you are familiar with Building Block #4, Contextual Learning and the Time Line, then you can cross reference here the first Two Great Turning Points of Creation of the Universe and Creation of Man. See Chapters #10 and #11 in The Manual for Contextual Learning, also called 'A Panoramic View of 6,000 Years.'

Man was created to exercise his freedom of choices in relation to his Middos.[7]

The entire world is really Hashem's Mind turning up in a person's life every moment, inviting him to exercise his bechira.[8] And what exactly is Bechira? Freedom of choice. But free-will appears so complex, is it possible that it is actually simple!?

The simple answer is a resounding YES! *Bechira is thought in the moment.*[9]

When you make a choice, it is a thought in the moment.

Even if your decision to do something came from many hours, days or even weeks and months of deliberation, the final decision is always a thought in that moment. The expression '*change of mind*' is so revealing in its terminology because it actually means "I had a thought and now I have changed my mind, because now I have a different thought."

---

7 Vilna Gaon, Even Sheleima, opening paragraph - 1:1 - כל עבודת ה' תלויה בתיקון המדות
8 Berachos 33b. הכל ביד שמים חוץ מיראת שמים - really means that we are all living inside a brilliantly designed Divine Illusion. Everything we see and experience is literally Hashem turning up in our minds in that moment. Our Bechira, Yiras Shamayim is all we own in responding to Hashem's Olam HaSheker and Olam HaDimion, brilliantly disguised as a real world!
9 Likutei Moharan II, Lesson 50 & 51, see also lesson 110. Chayey Moharan #44. See Shulchan Aruch Even HaEzer 38:31. Kiddushin 49b (the Rasha gamur who said to an Isha I am betrothed to you on condition I am a Tzadik Gamur is Mekudeshes because perhaps he had a thought of Teshuva in that moment.

1.2 When do children begin to learn Middos?

From birth! Almost all childhood experiences come from the adults in the child's life. His parents, teachers, extended family, grandparents, they all provide the role modeling for that child's own Middos in his formative years.

But the true Middos of a person are never etched in stone till his very last day when the full reckoning will be accounted for. Even if a person were wicked his entire life, but did Teshuva in the last moment, he has a portion in Olam Haba.[10]

The ultimate purpose of all areas of Chinuch have to point to the same end-goal, and that end-goal is *independence*.[11] Independence in Middos means the child is learning to control himself from inside out, not outside in. He is motivated from within. Not from incentives or even praise.[12] He does the right thing because it is the right thing. But that does not come naturally, it has to be role modeled.

Independence in Middos has to mean we let go of blaming and take responsibility for controlling oneself. A Baal Middos is independent because he sees his experiences and feelings as products of his thought and not other stimuli over which he has no control. Once Middos is all about thought, now begins the liberation from thinking one is controlled by people or circumstances.

---

10 Rambam Hilchos Teshuva, 3:14. Even one who was Kofer B'Ikar his whole life and at the very end of his life he did Teshuva, he has a portion in Olam Haba.

11 Kiddushin 29a. Chazal list the obligations of a parent to a child. Each one appears different, but they are all describing the same end goal, to nurture *independence* in the child. 1. Teach Torah (so he is his own *independent* link in the chain of the Mesora, he can learn Torah *independently* and can teach his children Torah). 2. Marry a wife (so he can start his own family). 3. Teach a trade (so he can be financially *independent*). 4. Teach your child to swim (so will be *independently* able to take of himself in time of need or danger).

12 When Chazal describe the need to give incentives to children, there is a descending order of motivation from external to internal. Stage 1 is food incentives, kilayos and Egozim. Stage 2 is to tell the child he will be respected for his learning status (people will give him Kavod for being so good at learning Torah). Stage 3 is to wean the child from the need for recognition and tell him the ultimate goal for learning is Lishma, for the sake of giving Hashem Nachas, for He commands us in this Mitzvah. So we see how there is a gradual weaning from external incentives as and when the child's mind has matured.

2.0 Will the Real You Please Stand Up!
You are Tzelem Elokim!

Who is the real me, the real you?
Your body?
Your clothes?
Your career?
Your possessions?
Your family?
The real you is the only part of you that is impossible to destroy, that lives forever, because it is Divine Intelligence in the form of your Tzelem Elokim.

What does that mean?

'Tzelem Elokim' literally means a 'reflection of unlimited power.'

Hashem created us in 'His Image,' a reflection of His unlimited powers[13] - וַיִּבְרָא אֱלֹקִים אֶת־הָאָדָם בְּצַלְמוֹ בְּצֶלֶם אֱלֹקִים בָּרָא אֹתוֹ - the Rishonim tell us the 'Tzelem Elokim' refers to the mind which itself is powered by our Neshama.[14]

Hashem created man with a body and soul[15] while in the description of man's demise, the Torah only mentions the body returning to where it came from, that is the earth,[16] but there is no mention of the soul dying because it is part of Hashem[17] and returns to Him, it is eternal, the real you is eternal!

You, the real you never dies!

---

13 Gen. 1:27.
14 See Sefer HaChinuch, Mitzvah #39 - מפני, שנתן באדם חלק השכל היא על "בצלמנו" שכתוב ומה"... "שהשכל כולו בו ברוך הוא." Also see Seforno on Gen.1:26 where he defines "בצלמנו" to be the "עצם שכלי ונצחי" - "the intrinsic eternal mind" in man infused from Hashem. You are created by Divine Intelligence, and your ability to think is powered by Divine Intelligence! See Likutei Moharan I, Torah #137 where this is even more clearly defined (and see the next Torah there #138), - ."שהחלק אלוקה ממעל שיש לי, אומר לי ומלמד אותי לשמור דבריך"
15 Gen.2:7 - וַיִּיצֶר ה' אֱלֹקִים אֶת־הָאָדָם עָפָר מִן־הָאֲדָמָה וַיִּפַּח בְּאַפָּיו נִשְׁמַת חַיִּים וַיְהִי הָאָדָם לְנֶפֶשׁ חַיָּה.
16 Gen. 3:19 - בְּזֵעַת אַפֶּיךָ תֹּאכַל לֶחֶם עַד שׁוּבְךָ אֶל־הָאֲדָמָה כִּי מִמֶּנָּה לֻקָּחְתָּ כִּי־עָפָר אַתָּה וְאֶל־עָפָר תָּשׁוּב.
17 The real you is your Soul, Neshama, called חלק אלוק ממעל (Iyov. 31:2, see Likutei Moharan I, Lesson #17:6, #137, #138 and in Tinyana (second volume) Lesson #10.

2.1 Let's Define Middos
The word מדה **means 'Character' and also means 'Measure!'**
A Baal Middos literally means the owner or master of measures! A Baal Middos means he is in control of his mind, and therefore his body and mouth too! The very word Midda means both 'measure' and 'character.' Why? Because the true *measure* of a human is his *character*. What else could be the true measure of a person? His height? His weight? The amount of money he makes? His job? How famous he is? How many letters at the end of his name? How many homes he owns? We all know the truth, the only true measure of any human throughout history is his Middos, character. All righteous behavior begins with Middos.

The very name for a Jew, 'Yehudi' and 'Yisrael' define us - a Yehudi comes from the lashon of Hoda'ah, gratitude and thus a Yehudi is really a 'Thank-you-er.' The essence of a Jew is he is a grateful person, full of gratitude to Hashem for choosing us from all the nations to be His righteous nation who exemplify His Torah and lifestyle through our Middos Tovos.

The other name for a Jew is Yisrael which is the combination of two words - 'Yashar-El,' which means **El**, The Only **Power** is yashar, righteous, honest, straight.

When we live with Middos Tovos, we automatically bring Kavod to Hashem. Through our exemplary Middos, people will say 'Hashem is Yashar' - Yashar El - ישר-אל.

24,000 students of Rebi Akiva died because they were not careful with their inter-personal relationships, their Middos bein adam l'chavero.
שלא נזהרו בכבוד חבריהם

זהירות correctly translates as *clarity, awareness*. We often translate זהירות as careful, but that is the end product of Zehirus. The process to reach *carefulness* is *clarity* and *awareness* in the first place that I am not treating you with respect.

זהיר comes from the root word זהר which means *shine*, or a *shining light*. Thus, when you *shine clarity* on an issue you become much more *aware* and thus more *careful*.

כבד - כבוד The word Kavod, honor, appreciation, dignity, comes from the three letter root Kaved, 'heavy.' Other people's dignity is a weighty, heavy matter, not to be taken lightly.
You can only be careful for something you have awareness of.

You cannot be careful to eat with good manners if you are not aware of what is good manners!

You cannot dress well if you are not aware you look like a shloch. After you look in the mirror you might be aware, or if someone you respect helps you see your clothes are undignified, you can make a change.

Self-Awareness must come before self-control and self-management. A Baal Middos has to first know what is the Midda he wants to emulate.

2.2 Can Middos be taught?

So how do we help children be aware of their behavior or lack of Middos?

Essentially, there is always one same answer, show children how to behave!

Middos can be learned only through role modeling.

וְשִׁנַּנְתָּם לְבָנֶיךָ[18]

Repeat to *your children* - these are *your students*.

What are you repeating? - That *Hashem is The Only One Power of all powers!* and you are also repeating the Mitzvah of Ahavas Hashem. This is what you are role modeling as a parent and teacher in the Mitzvah of וְשִׁנַּנְתָּם לְבָנֶיךָ![19]

This means teaching Middos is more about the *spiritual work of the teacher* than how to discipline the child!

2.3. Identify the Core mechanic of all Middos.

Daas, Mind/thought.

Paying attention = Awareness. If a child is not aware of how he is reading faster than he can properly read, swallowing entire words and syllables as he 'reads,' it is because he is not *aware* of his lack of accuracy and fluency. Why is he not aware? Because he is not *paying attention* to the letters and Nekudos.

Why is the teenager not *aware* that Mum has called him several times to dinner? Because his mind is so absorbed in the game he is playing, he is not *paying attention* to anything else!

Why is my spouse not *aware* of his weaknesses? Because he is not *paying attention*.

To have awareness of my Middos, I have to pay attention to the source of my Middos. The source of my Middos is thought in the moment.

---

18 Dev. 6:7. וְשִׁנַּנְתָּם לְבָנֶיךָ וְדִבַּרְתָּ - The Sifri says 'to your children' refers to your students (cited in Rashi there - לְבָנֶיךָ. אֵלּוּ הַתַּלְמִידִים. מָצִינוּ בְּכָל מָקוֹם שֶׁהַתַּלְמִידִים קְרוּיִים בָּנִים, שֶׁנֶּאֱמַר "בָּנִים אַתֶּם לַה' אֱלֹהֵיכֶם" (דברים יד:א)

19 See last Tosafot in Brachos 13a who identifies these as the core message of Shema.

2.4 The True Body-Mind-Emotion Dynamic.

We feel what we think 100% of the time.
It is impossible to experience life any other way. We always feel what we are thinking. No exceptions.

That's why לב means both *thought* and *heart*.

You can only ever feel what you are thinking.

Lev has to mean both. Hashem deliberately designed us to more easily experience the 'feeling of emotion' in order for us to have a window into what we are thinking! We can only feel what we think. This is a simple incontrovertible law. Everyone who ever lived experiences life the exact same way, through thought in the moment. Whatever we feel is what we are thinking right then and there.

So the entire purpose of all our emotions is to tell us what we are thinking!

Your emotions are G-d's design to help you know the true and only source of your emotions!

2.5 Define Lev.

The word 'Lev' has 4 meanings[20], but for the purpose of this discussion, we are focused on just two, which are *mind* and *heart*.[21]

Examples of Lev = Mind-Thought-Emotion
1. Love Hashem with all your thoughts - Dev. 6:5[22]
2. Don't hate your brother in your thoughts - Lev. 19:17[23]
3. Don't trust your thoughts - Num. 15:39[24]
4. Cut out your negative thinking - Dev. 10:16[25]
5. Know today and repeat it in your thoughts that - Only Hashem exists - Dev. 4:39

It is precisely because *we only ever feel what we think*, that the word לב has to mean both *thought* and the *icon of emotion*.

You simply cannot separate the two.

You immediately feel whatever you are thinking.

The simple explanation for why Hashem made us function this way is because thought is extremely elusive, we easily forget that we only live in thought all the time, we don't pay attention to it!

Thought is similar to oxygen. How often do you think about the air your breath? Almost never! Even though you are breathing air every second of your life! Oxygen is everywhere all the time, so you never need to think about it!

---

20 For example, Gen.6:3 וַיַּרְא ה' כִּי רַבָּה רָעַת הָאָדָם בָּאָרֶץ וְכָל־יֵצֶר מַחְשְׁבֹת לִבּוֹ רַק רַע כָּל־הַיּוֹם - Lev means *mind*. See also Mishley 19:21 - רַבּוֹת מַחֲשָׁבוֹת בְּלֶב־אִישׁ. In Ex. 15:8 - Lev is a *metaphor*, - קָפְאוּ וְהָרוּ בֹעֵר בְּאֵשׁ עַד־לֵב -Lev is a metaphor, - תְהֹמֹת בְּלֶב־יָם the 'heart of the sea.' So too Dev. 4:11 הַשָּׁמַיִם - 'the heart of the heavens.' In Ex. 28:29-30, Lev means the *physical heart* as with the Hoshen *against the heart* of Aron Kohen Gadol - וְנָשָׂא אַהֲרֹן אֶת־שְׁמוֹת בְּנֵי־יִשְׂרָאֵל בְּחֹשֶׁן הַמִּשְׁפָּט עַל־לִבּוֹ.
21 We mean *heart* as the icon of *emotion*.
22 See Ibn Ezra and Ramban on Dev.6:5 who define Lev as DAAT. Their exact wording is לב הוא הדעת.
23 Knowing that hatred is actually thought, is a huge help in understanding how the Torah can tell us to control an emotion, because the Torah is telling us to notice the origin of our hatred, the true source is thought of hate in the moment. We are always in control of our next thought in the moment! So Hashem says don't have thoughts of hate and if I notice such thoughts surface in my mind, then ignore them because they are forbidden and Hashem says I can let go of them.
24 All Rishonim agree this Passuk וְלֹא תָתוּרוּ אַחֲרֵי לְבַבְכֶם וְאַחֲרֵי עֵינֵיכֶם is one of the Taryag Mitzvos and it applies every second of our lives. The same verse already told us to remember all 613 Mitzvos, the connection being that I have to remember all the Mitzvos so that I know what to think and what not to think! The Torah gives us Mitzvos of the Mind.
25 Radak in Sefer HaSherashim defines ערלה as a lashon of מיותר - extra. So now the verse reads ומלתם את ערלת לבבכם - Remove your extra thinking! What are extra, unnecessary thoughts? Any thoughts the Torah tells me to avoid! Hate, revenge, desire for other people's possessions, Kina - Jealousy, Taava, Kavod, bearing a grudge, not judging others favorably. All these are Mitzvos of the mind and the Torah is telling me which thoughts to cut out! They are all Non-Reality! Anger, Jealousy and hate are misjudgments. They are not reality thinking. In fact, Chazal even tell us (Avot 4:21) that such thinking takes me out of reality, out of this world - רַבִּי אֶלְעָזָר הַקַּפָּר אוֹמֵר, הַקִּנְאָה וְהַתַּאֲוָה וְהַכָּבוֹד מוֹצִיאִין אֶת הָאָדָם מִן הָעוֹלָם.

Thought is even closer to you than air! You are only able to have an experience because you think!

We think every moment of our waking hours, minutes and seconds, so we don't see a need to *think about thought!* We 'do' thinking all the time!

We constantly fall into the illusion that *the world is acting upon us.* So, it must be the world happening to us that appears to be the origin of our feelings. That is the outside-in paradigm. This is why Chazal call this world Olam HaDimion and Olam HaSheker. We are all living inside a Divine Illusion!

Feelings are much more recognizable than thought. So Hashem gave us emotions in order for us to identify what we are thinking.

Knowing what we are thinking by paying attention to our feelings is what gives us the measure to know if we are living with Hashem or not! Feelings are flags directing me to know if we are following what Hashem wants me to think. Are we in 'Reality-Thinking' or 'Non-Reality-Thinking?' Are my thoughts saturated with the Yetzer Hara or Yetzer HaTov?

This is the simple meaning of רחמנה לבא בעי,[26] 'Hashem wants the mind,' meaning, *the **true you** is your thought in the moment*, and Hashem wants us to have Him in our thoughts. This concept is echoed throughout TaNaCh and Poskim.

For example, Chazal ask which one verse encapsulates the essence of the Torah?[27] They answer בְּכָל־דְּרָכֶיךָ דָעֵהוּ - '*In all your ways acknowledge Him.*'

The opening words of the Rema in Shulchan Aruch is a quote from Tehilim 16:8 שִׁוִּיתִי ה' לְנֶגְדִּי תָמִיד - where the Rema elaborates that all our behavior should be mindful of Hashem's Presence with us. It is all about what we are thinking.

Later in Shulchan Aruch, Orach Chaim,[28] an entire section is dedicated to 'how to think' in whatever we do, whether it be Mitzvos, or eating, drinking, walking, talking, etc.[29] The Mechaber tells us all our actions should be with the intent to serve Hashem, live with Hashem in your thought! In doing so, claims the author of Shulchan

---

26 Sanhedrin 106a.
27 דרש בר קפרא: איזוהי פרשה קטנה שכל גופי תורה תלוין בה - (משלי ג:ו) **בכל דרכיך דעהו** והוא יישר ארחתיך.
28 Siman #231
29 The very title of the Siman (231) is - שכל כוונותיו יהיו לשם שמים

Aruch, one can literally serve Hashem all the time because it all depends on what we are thinking! *Hashem gave us feelings so we can be immediately aware of our thoughts*, and thus know if we are living with Hashem in mind or not!

Now let's redefine Middos as '***Laws of the Mind!***' We will look briefly at each Midda and categorize each one under ***Reality or Non-Reality Thinking***.

Another way of putting this is:
How We Experience Life & How We Do Not!
How *it* (*it* = all experiences and feelings) works and how *it* does not work.

We are our Minds.[30] Our Middos are shaped by our thoughts. When we leave this world, the sum total of our life will be largely measured by our intent behind what we said and did. In many Mitzvos of the Torah, Hashem signs off "'ויראת מאלקיך אני ה'" to remind us that He knows what we are thinking when we do that Mitzvah.[31] Thought is everything!

The list below of the Mitzvos of the Mind is intended to imbue in you, the reader, the extraordinary emphasis the Torah puts on 'paying attention' to our very thoughts.

So many Mitzvos depend on what we are thinking in the moment, it is literally a matter of eternal life to increase this awareness.

We have written many footnotes for each Midda for you to see how much our lives are really all about thought.

Please take advantage of reading the footnotes to reinforce this message till you, yourself experience more and more insights into your own patterns of thought.

The moment you truly experience how life takes place inside-out and never really outside in, you will begin to experience a liberation from thoughts of anger, accusations, complaints, resentment, or worse, thoughts of revenge and self-pity.

You will be inspired to work on this for yourself and your students.

---

30 See Likutey Halachos, Hilchos Birkas Hariah, Birkas Pratiot, Halacha 5.
וזה לשונו - עיקר האדם הוא המחשבה שֶׁבַּמֹּחַ שֶׁהִיא הנשמה

31 See Lev. 19:14 - 'ה - וְיָרֵאתָ מֵּאֱלֹהֶיךָ אֲנִי Rashi - (Citing Toraas Kohanim 7:4) - וְיָרֵאתָ מֵּאֱלֹהֶיךָ. לְפִי שֶׁהַדָּבָר הַזֶּה אֵינוֹ מָסוּר לַבְּרִיּוֹת לֵידַע אִם דַּעְתּוֹ שֶׁל זֶה לְטוֹבָה אוֹ לְרָעָה, וְיָכוֹל לְהִשָּׁמֵט וְלוֹמַר לְטוֹבָה נִתְכַּוַּנְתִּי, לְפִיכָךְ נֶאֱמַר בּוֹ "וְיָרֵאתָ מֵּאֱלֹהֶיךָ", הַמַּכִּיר מַחְשְׁבוֹתֶיךָ, וְכֵן כָּל דָּבָר הַמָּסוּר לְלִבּוֹ שֶׁל אָדָם הָעוֹשֵׂהוּ, וְאֵין שְׁאָר הַבְּרִיּוֹת מַכִּירוֹת בּוֹ, נֶאֱמַר בּוֹ "וְיָרֵאתָ מֵּאֱלֹהֶיךָ".

2.6 Hilchos Middos is Hilchos Thinking!
We will now look at the Thoughts (and thus the Middos) the Torah commands us to imbue in our character as well as those thoughts the Torah instructs us to avoid.

Middos of the Mind really fall into two categories:

1. **Reality-Thinking** - (RT) How we truly experience life, always.
2. **Non-Reality-Thinking** - (NR) How life is not truly experienced.

Examples of Reality Thoughts would be Love of Hashem, Yirat Hashem, love for others.

2.7 Middos in Taryag Mitzvos.

The list below is a compilation of Mitzvos listed in Rambam, SmaG, SMaK, Ramban and Sefer Chareidim. Each Midda in this list is counted as one of the Taryag Mitzvos by at least one of these Rishonim. **They are all Mitzvos of the Mind.**

These are literally the thoughts Hashem is commanding all of us to either think or avoid. The Non-Reality-Thoughts are the illusion provided by the Yetzer Hara, while the Reality-Thoughts are the Yetzer Tov.

After each Mitzvah we have written either **R** for a 'Reality-Thought or **NRT** for a **N**one-**R**eality-**T**hought.

1. Ahavas Hashem.[32]   R
2. Ahavas Yisrael.[33]   R
3. Ahavas HaGer.[34]   R
4. Hatred.[35]   NR
5. Jealousy.   NR[36]

---

[32] Dev. 6:5 - וְאָהַבְתָּ אֵת ה' אֱלֹקֶיךָ בְּכָל־לְבָבְךָ וּבְכָל־נַפְשְׁךָ וּבְכָל־מְאֹדֶךָ - The Mitzvah to Love Hashem is a Mitzvah of the Mind and applies every waking second of our lives. The Torah instructs us to Love Hashem with all our thoughts - בְּכָל־לְבָבְךָ, which Chazal (Brachos 9:5) tell us refers to love Hashem with both the Yetzer Tov and Yetzer Hara. The Yetzer Tov and Yetzer Hara are both thoughts (see Likutei Moharan I, Lesson #49 where he writes - המחשבות טובות הם היצר טוב והמחשבות רעות הם היצר הרע. So when you have Yetzer Hara thought and you ignore it, you are showing your love for Hashem in that moment. When a thought of jealousy pops into your mind and you decide not to think about it, you are loving Hashem with your Yetzer Hara. When you have a thought of resentment (נטירה) or hatred (שנאה) and you ignore these thoughts, you are loving Hashem with your Yetzer Hara.

[33] Lev. 19:18 - וְאָהַבְתָּ לְרֵעֲךָ כָּמוֹךָ - Love every Jew, this includes your parents, your siblings, your friends, your teachers, your neighbor, love work, love gentiles and love all creatures (Avot 1:12)

[34] Dev. 10:19 - וַאֲהַבְתֶּם אֶת־הַגֵּר - Love a convert to Judaism. This Mitzvah is done with your thoughts. Every time you think about a virtue in this Ger Tzedek (he decided to join Beney Yisrael on his or her own volition) you get this Mitzvah. Love starts as a thought.

[35] Lev. 19:17 - לֹא־תִשְׂנָא אֶת־אָחִיךָ בִּלְבָבֶךָ - means to not hate your brother in your thoughts. Though almost all our translations innocently follow the popular translation of 'don't hate your brother in your heart' it cannot be accurate because the word בִּלְבָבֶךָ should then translate as 'in your hearts' since it is plural. That would not make sense because a person only has one heart. The correct meaning is 'thoughts.' See Ibn Ezra & Ramban on Dev. 6:5 on the words 'love Hashem with all your thoughts' they write three words הלב הוא הדעת, the word Lev is the Mind. Once you translate the word Lev correctly as mind or thought, literally hundreds of Passukim make more logical sense. As we explained, the moment you think something, you feel it. You feel your thoughts all the time. One hundred percent of your feelings are thought in the moment, always. So Hashem designed us to *feel our thinking* so we would know the true source of our feelings are thought in the moment. It can never be any other way because this is reality, period! Now we understand that not to hate another Jew means be aware of thoughts of *hatred* and now you have the Mitzvah to delete such a thought by not thinking about it in your next thoughts.

[36] All Rishonim agree Jealousy is a Mitzvah of the mind. The Torah defines two types of jealousy. Each on is counted as a separate Lo Taaseh of Taryag Mitzvos. One type is לֹא־תִתְאַוֶּה - which refers to a thought of jealousy where you plan how to get the item you are jealous of. This is in Ex. 20:13 - לֹא תַחְמֹד בֵּית רֵעֶךָ לֹא־תַחְמֹד אֵשֶׁת רֵעֶךָ וְעַבְדּוֹ וַאֲמָתוֹ וְשׁוֹרוֹ וַחֲמֹרוֹ וְכֹל אֲשֶׁר לְרֵעֶךָ. The second type of jealousy is simply the thought of jealousy without planning to get that item belonging to

6. Respect.[37] R
7. Simcha.[38] R
8. Patience.[39] R
9. Emuna.[40] R
10 Hashem is Echad.[41] R

---

someone else. This is called לֹא תִתְאַוֶּה - and is found in the second description of the Aseres Hadibros in Dev. 5:18 וְלֹא תִתְאַוֶּה בֵּית רֵעֶךָ שָׂדֵהוּ וְעַבְדּוֹ וַאֲמָתוֹ שׁוֹרוֹ וַחֲמֹרוֹ וְכֹל אֲשֶׁר לְרֵעֶךָ. Though we have listed jealousy as Non-Reality-Thinking, if jealousy is used to motivate one to be better without diminishing one's love and respect for the person one is jealous of (and does not want them to lose what you are jealous of) then that would be considered Reality-Thinking, and a good use of jealousy. This idea of positive jealousy is found in Orchot Tzadikim, Shaar Kina where he gives examples of positive jealousy, such as Rachel had for her twin sister Leah (Gen. 30:1 - וַתֵּרֶא רָחֵל כִּי לֹא יָלְדָה לְיַעֲקֹב וַתְּקַנֵּא רָחֵל בַּאֲחֹתָהּ - see Rashi who quotes Chazal that her jealousy was born from seeing Leah's excellent character and kind actions, it was not that she wanted what Leah had and that Leah would no longer have what Rachel was jealous of, Hass Veshalom - תִּקְנֵא רָחֵל בַּאֲחֹתָהּ. קִנְאָה בְּמַעֲשֶׂיהָ הַטּוֹבִים, אָמְרָה, אִלּוּלֵי שֶׁצַּדְקָה מִמֶּנִּי לֹא זָכְתָה לְבָנִים -

37 See Sefer Chareidim, Mitzvas Aseh #17 to fear one's parents, he includes in this Mitzvah having respect for parents in-law, older brother and all older siblings of both genders, his step-mother, step father, all Talmidei Chachamim, beney Torah and all Yirei Hashem. Ben Ish Chai (Parshas Ki Tavo, Second Chelek, Halacha #12 includes any elderly person above the age of 70. He adds that the Arizal writes that one should stand for a Zaken who is 60 years and over and recommends one follow the Arizal.

38 Dev. 28:47 - תַּחַת אֲשֶׁר לֹא־עָבַדְתָּ אֶת־ה' אֱלֹקֶיךָ בְּשִׂמְחָה וּבְטוּב לֵבָב מֵרֹב כֹּל - (all these curses will come upon you) because you did not serve Hashem with Simcha with good thoughts from the abundance of everything good while you had it." See Rashi who explains that while we had all Hashem's blessings, we were not happy! Happiness is a choice to enjoy the good already in our lives. The verse is informing us of the underlying reason for suffering, we did not enjoy being frum Jews! See also Dev. 28:11 וְשָׂמַחְתָּ בְּכָל־הַטּוֹב אֲשֶׁר נָתַן־לְךָ ה' אֱלֹקֶיךָ - "Be happy with all the good Hashem your Power has gifted you." See also Tehilim 100:2 - עִבְדוּ אֶת־יְהוָה בְּשִׂמְחָה - "serve Happiness in happiness." The word for 'thought' in Lashon HaKodesh is מחשבה. The word for being in the state of joy is בשמחה. The two words share the exact same letters! Because happiness is a thought (I heard this in the name of the Arizal but do not know the source). The Baal Shem HaKadosh offers a similar insight, the root word for happiness is שמח which is a combination of two words, the first two letters spell שם and the last two letter spell - מח meaning Simcha is 'there in the mind.' Likutei Moharan often writes that source of Simcha is in the Lev, in the mind, as David HaMelech wrote (Tehilim 4:8) נָתַתָּה שִׂמְחָה בְלִבִּי - You have already gifted happiness in my mind." Meaning, all the reason to be happy are already in our mind. We already have the gift of joy. All we have to do is count our blessings, the kindness Hashem does for us all the time from the moment we were born till now, and for all our family and all Klal Yisrael. Then we will realize Happiness is a constant gift, it is always inside us for the taking! (see Likutei Moharan, I, lesson #282 and in volume II, lessons #10 and #17. See also Likutei Moharan II, Lesson #24 - מצוה גדולה להיות בשמחה תמיד. Orchos Tzadikim counts the Mitzvah of Happiness in doing a Mitzvah as worth 1000 times more than a Mitzvah done without Simcha (Shaar Simcha).

39 Ex. 34:6 - 13 Middos of Rachamim, includes Erech Apayim, patience. We are commanded to Emulate Hashem (Dev.28:9) which includes emulating all these Middos. See #9 in this list 'To go in Hashem's ways.'

40 Ex. 20:2 - All Rishonim agree the Mitzvah of Emuna in Hashem is a Mitzvah of the mind and applies every waking moment of our lives. Emuna means we know in our thoughts that Hashem is the Supervisor of every detail in history. Hashem instructs us to have Emuna, faith and even certainty that He Alone governs events in a perfectly calculated method of Midda Keneged Midda. He never makes a mistake as He describes about Himself in Dev. 32:4 הַצּוּר תָּמִים פָּעֳלוֹ כִּי כָל־דְּרָכָיו מִשְׁפָּט קֵל אֱמוּנָה וְאֵין עָוֶל צַדִּיק וְיָשָׁר הוּא. Habakuk the Prophet, famously claimed that if you select one Mitzvah to encapsulate all the other 612 Mitzvot, it would be the Mitzvah of Emuna (Makkot 24a - בא חבקוק והעמידן על אחת, שנאמר: (חבקוק ב') וצדיק באמונתו יחיה. See Tehilim 119:86 - כָּל־מִצְוֺתֶיךָ אֱמוּנָה - 'All your Mitzvos are Emuna.' See there Ibn Ezra that all Your Mitzvos are for me to live with Emuna.

11. Judge others favorably.[42]	R
12. Onas Devarim.[43]	NR
13. Lashon Hara & Rechilus.[44]	NR
14. Don't remember other people's mistakes.[45]	NR

---

[41] Dev.6:4 - Hashem is the Only Power in the universe. This is one of the few Passukim that are part of our daily Tefila, a verbal declaration in Shema Yisrael. This Mitzvah has to be done with our thoughts engaged in the words otherwise the declaration has to be repeated (Shulchan Aruch, orach Chaim, 60:5).

[42] This is a Mitzvah of the mind. Judging others is a thought. The Torah instructs us to look for a favorable interpretation of a person's behavior which would otherwise be understood as bad. Lev. 19:15 - בְּצֶדֶק תִּשְׁפֹּט עֲמִיתֶךָ. The Rishonim define this Mitzvah as applicable to both Dayanim and laymen. Dayanim have the Mitzvah not to show more favor to one litigant over the other, while for the layman, this Mitzvah is the command to judge others favorably. See also Avot 1:6 וֶהֱוֵי דָן אֶת כָּל הָאָדָם לְכַף זְכוּת. The message here is that judging others takes place in the mind and is thus a thought in the moment. To judge unfavorably is not reality because we never know all the factors in another person's life to be able to judge them honestly. Only Hashem can do that (Avot 4:8 - אַל תְּהִי דָן יְחִידִי, שֶׁאֵין דָּן יְחִידִי אֶלָּא אֶחָד). Hashem never asked me to be other people's policeman! If I have a halachic claim against another, then a Dayan has the responsibility to judge between us based on all available evidence. But outside of Bais Din, Hashem wants us to work things out between each other, and that begins with thought! What am I thinking that is making me upset with someone else? Be aware of where I am thinking judgmental thoughts because the Torah clearly instructs me to think good of you! Another obvious source for not judging others altogether is Avot 2:4 'Don't judge your friend till you are in his place' - וְאַל תָּדִין אֶת חֲבֵרְךָ עַד שֶׁתַּגִּיעַ לִמְקוֹמוֹ. But will you ever be in his exact place, inside his shoes? Never! So Chazal are describing another way of saying 'just don't judge!'

[43] Don't hurt others with words. Though the Issur is not to say unkind and hurtful words, insults, curse words, etc, the Mitzvah starts in the mind. Rashi there points this out. This Mitzvah is from Lev. 25:17 - וְלֹא תוֹנוּ אִישׁ אֶת־עֲמִיתוֹ וְיָרֵאתָ מֵאֱלֹקֶיךָ כִּי אֲנִי ה' אֱלֹקֵיכֶם. Rashi gives examples of causing pain with words and includes in this Issur giving harmful advice. He then cites Toras Kohanim 2 and Bava Metzia 58b who derive from fact that Hashem ends the verse with "you shall fear Hashem Your Power' is as though Hashem warns us not to harm others with words and claim one did not intend to hurt them *because I know all your thoughts*! Rashi - מִי יֹאמַר, וְאִם תֹּאמַר יוֹדֵעַ אִם נִתְכַּוַּנְתִּי לְרָעָה, לְכָךְ נֶאֱמַר "וְיָרֵאתָ מֵאֱלֹקֶיךָ", הַיּוֹדֵעַ מַחֲשָׁבוֹת הוּא יוֹדֵעַ, כָּל דָּבָר הַמָּסוּר לַלֵּב, שֶׁאֵין מַכִּיר אֶלָּא מִי שֶׁהַמַּחֲשָׁבָה בְלִבּוֹ, נֶאֱמַר בּוֹ "וְיָרֵאתָ מֵאֱלֹקֶיךָ". - from Rashi's words, you can see that thought in the Lev refers to this Mitzvah being sourced in thought.

[44] The issur not to gossip is learned from Lev. 19:16 - לֹא־תֵלֵךְ רָכִיל בְּעַמֶּיךָ - 'Don't go gossiping amongst your people.' While the Issur not to say Lashon Hara is learned from Lev. 23:1 - לֹא תִשָּׂא שֵׁמַע שָׁוְא - from where Chazal derive not to speak or accept Lashon Hara. The literal reading is 'Don't elevate wasted listening.' (the words לֹא תִשָּׂא literally mean 'don't lift up' or 'don't elevate.' The words שֵׁמַע שָׁוְא means 'listening for nothing' or as we are translating, 'wasted listening'). The Issur of Lashon Hara and Rechilus really start in our mind. The more we love someone, the harder it is to hear negative about them. A parent who loves his child finds it hard to hear negative about their child. The Issur to listen and accept Lashon Hara is also a Mitzvah of the mind because it is in my thoughts that I have to reject listening to Lashon Hara and it is also in my thought where the very desire to speak negatively about someone originates.

[45] Hashem would never instruct a Mitzvah which is impossible to fulfil. Every Mitzvah and Lo Taaseh is by default Hashem's vote of confidence that we can fulfil this Mitzvah. G-d trusts us because He created us with the inner strength to overcome our grudges against others. This Lo Taaseh is translated from Lev. 19:18 - וְלֹא־תִטֹּר אֶת־בְּנֵי עַמֶּךָ - as 'Don't bare a grudge (against members of your people).' As the Gemora in Yuma 23a points out, this is a command not to remember other people's mistakes and hold it against them. Rashi there defines לֹא־תִטֹּר as a Lashon of נטירה - guarding, ונוטר - איבה כנחש בלבו 'like a snake who has איבה - deep seated hatred in his Lev.' Rashi further elaborates on the word נטירה - שהדבר שמור בלבו, ולא הסיחו מדעתו - 'the item is guarded in his Lev and does not remove it from his mind.' In other words, don't guard in your mind the memories of other people's mistakes against you, instead, remove them from your mind.' This Mitzvah of the Mind is huge! So much of our lives, head space, is taken up with memories of what is wrong in life, what we do not like about so and so or the weather, or the circumstances or job or neighbors, etc, etc. Hashem makes a simple instruction to pay attention to my emotion so I can know what I am thinking! Then I become aware of when I am holding

15. Don't take revenge.⁴⁶   NR
16. Remember Hashem's kindness.⁴⁷   R
17. Teshuva.⁴⁸   R
18. Tamim, be completely trusting in Hashem.⁴⁹   R

---

onto negative memories instead of dumping them! Instead of deleting them! How? By not thinking about that person's faults! Even when the memory of their 'crime' against you pops up, hey! It is only a thought in the moment and you are always one thought away from the next thought, which Rashi tells us 'just let go' - don't hold onto that thought, let go! - **שהדבר שמור בלבו, ולא הסיחו מדעתו**. How can you let go if the thought seems so overpowering? Thank Hashem, praise Him for your negative thought of resentment because now you can serve Him by ignoring the thought! Thank Hashem for your Yetzer Hara pop-up because now you can show your love for Hashem by letting go of the Netira, resentful thoughts. Hashem is so certain of His request that should we ever think it is beyond us to let go of negative memories, Hashem signs His Name at the end of the same verse - **אני ה'**, as though to say - "I know you can overcome your desire to remember negative memories because I Am the One Who designed your mind!"

46   The Mitzvah not to take revenge is counted as a Mitzvah of the Mind by Sefer Chareidim - (Ch.#21. Paragraph 20-21). It is one of three Mitzvos in the same verse in Lev. 19:18 - **לֹא־תִקֹּם וְלֹא־תִטֹּר אֶת־בְּנֵי עַמֶּךָ וְאָהַבְתָּ לְרֵעֲךָ כָּמוֹךָ אֲנִי ה'** - 'don't take **revenge**, don't **remember other people's mistakes** and **love others** as yourself, I Am Hashem.' All three Mitzvos are of the Mind (Sefer Chareidim) they start inside your thought.

47   Dev. 8:2-5 - **וְזָכַרְתָּ אֶת־כָּל־הַדֶּרֶךְ אֲשֶׁר הוֹלִיכְךָ ה' אֱלֹהֶיךָ זֶה אַרְבָּעִים שָׁנָה בַּמִּדְבָּר... שִׂמְלָתְךָ לֹא בָלְתָה מֵעָלֶיךָ וְרַגְלְךָ לֹא בָצֵקָה זֶה אַרְבָּעִים שָׁנָה** and Dev. 8:18 - **וְזָכַרְתָּ אֶת־ה' אֱלֹהֶיךָ כִּי הוּא הַנֹּתֵן לְךָ כֹּחַ לַעֲשׂוֹת חָיִל**. The Ben Ish Chai, (Chelek Bais, Parshas Ekev) writes - **על מצוה יסוד וקיום העולם כולה שחושק אדם תמיד** - 'The foundational Mitzvah that sustains the entire world is Man's constant yearning (for Hashem) born from his awareness that all he ever understands is (a gift) from Hashem and not generated by himself.' **כל הטובה אשר ישיג בעולם הזה שהם מאת השם יתברך ולא ממנו עצמו.**
Also, see Sefer Chareidim, Aseh #16 of the Mind - **מצוה עשה לזכור תמיד זכרון חסדי ה' ואשר עשה עם אבותינו כמו שכתוב: וְזָכַרְתָּ אֶת־כָּל־הַדֶּרֶךְ אֲשֶׁר הוֹלִיכְךָ ה' אֱלֹהֶיךָ זֶה אַרְבָּעִים שָׁנָה בַּמִּדְבָּר לְמַעַן עַנֹּתְךָ לְנַסֹּתְךָ לָדַעַת אֶת־אֲשֶׁר בִּלְבָבְךָ הֲתִשְׁמֹר מִצְוֹתָיו אִם־לֹא: ג וַיְעַנְּךָ וַיַּרְעִבֶךָ וַיַּאֲכִלְךָ אֶת־הַמָּן אֲשֶׁר לֹא־יָדַעְתָּ וְלֹא יָדְעוּן אֲבֹתֶיךָ לְמַעַן הוֹדִיעֲךָ כִּי לֹא עַל־הַלֶּחֶם לְבַדּוֹ יִחְיֶה הָאָדָם כִּי עַל־כָּל־מוֹצָא פִי־ה': ד שִׂמְלָתְךָ לֹא בָלְתָה מֵעָלֶיךָ וְרַגְלְךָ לֹא בָצֵקָה זֶה אַרְבָּעִים שָׁנָה**. Sefer Chareidim adds that we should add to this our constant gratitude to Hashem for all He has done for Klal Yisrael ever since He took us out of Mitzrayim, and how much more so, to be additionally grateful on a personal level for His constant kindness with oneself from the day we were born!

48   Num. 5:7. The very word Teshuva means 'change' and 'return.' It refers to a change of direction from going away from Hashem and now returning to Him. The expression throughout Chazal of **הרהר תשובה בלבו** indicates that Teshuva begins with a thought in the mind. Shulchan Aruch offers a most extreme example of how far one thought of Teshuva affects Halacha. In Even HaEzer, 38:31, the case is quoted (from Kiddushin 49b) of Rasha Gamur, totally wicked man saying to a lady - "you are betrothed to me with this coin on condition I am a Tzadik Gamur (Hagaos R'Akiva Eiger), the marriage is valid because perhaps he had a thought of Teshuva! The Shulchan Aruch uses the language of **הרי זו מקודשת, שמא הרהר תשובה בלבו**. Interestingly, the source for this Halacha in the same case in the Gemora has the following wording - **הרי זו מקודשת, שמא הרהר תשובה בדעתו** - so you see that the word Lev means Daas, Mind. This is the power of Teshuva, a single thought in a moment of Teshuva can turn a Rasha Gamur into a Tzadik Gamur! Though the ultimate proof of Teshuva will be in a person not doing the Aveira again, nevertheless, the very thought alone is counted in Hashem's dictionary as binding. Another example of Teshuva being described in the mind is the verse in Dev. 30:14 where Moshe Rabeinu is encouraging us in the Mitzvah of Torah and Teshuva (see Berachos 17a - The Tachlis of Torah is Teshuva) - **כִּי־קָרוֹב אֵלֶיךָ הַדָּבָר מְאֹד בְּפִיךָ וּבִלְבָבְךָ לַעֲשׂוֹתוֹ** - 'This (Torah and Teshuva) is extremely close to you, in your mouth and your thoughts to act upon.' Sefer Chareidim counts Teshuva as a Mitzvah of the Mind.

49   Sefer Chareidim counts the Mitzvah to be Tamim as a Mitzvah of the Mind and is one of the 613 in his counting. It is derived from Dev. 18:13 - **תָּמִים תִּהְיֶה עִם ה' אֱלֹהֶיךָ**. Rashi elaborates that this Mitzvah instructs us to 'be completely trusting in Hashem.' These are the words of the Sifri (Paragraph #173) as cited in Rashi there - **תָּמִים תִּהְיֶה עִם ה' אֱלֹהֶיךָ. הִתְהַלֵּךְ עִמּוֹ בִּתְמִימוּת וּתְצַפֶּה לוֹ וְלֹא תַחֲקוֹר אַחַר הָעֲתִידוֹת, אֶלָּא כָּל מַה שֶׁיָּבֹא עָלֶיךָ קַבֵּל בִּתְמִימוּת, וְאָז תִּהְיֶה עִמּוֹ וּלְחֶלְקוֹ** - 'Walk with Hashem

19. Don't enter into Machlokes.⁵⁰	NR
20. Be Grateful⁵¹ - Live in a state of gratitude.	R

in complete trust, expect His salvation and don't speculate the future. Instead, accept whatever happens to you with complete trust (that Hashem is The One Source behind everything - Rashi Kepshuto) and then you will be with Hashem and (you will be counted as) in His Portion. See also Ramban, Ibn Ezra and Ohr HaChaim there. The main point is that all agree that being a Tam, completely trusting in Hashem, is a Mitzvah of the Mind. It refers to being so completely trusting that you absolutely know and trust Hashem in whatever happens to you. If you accept all that happens to you with Simcha and Ahava because you know this is from Hashem and therefore what He wants, it's His Ratzon, then you need not speculate why Hashem does what He does because He only does good always (see Biur Targum Yonatan Ben Uziel on this Passuk in Oz V'Hadar Edition of Mikraos Gedolos). The Ohr HaChaim also adds that this Mitzvah to be a Tam with Hashem is what can literally change your Mazal from bad to good. He proves it from Avraham Avinu who was not physically capable of fathering children (Shabbos 156b) but because he fulfilled Hashem's command in Gen. 17:1 - אֲנִי־קֵל שַׁקַּי הִתְהַלֵּךְ לְפָנַי וֶהְיֵה תָמִים, Avraham was able to transcend his Mazal and it changed so that he did father a son. Rashi understands Hashem's command to Avraham to be a Tam as to be totally trusting in Hashem in all the tests He sends him - וְהָיָה תָמִים. הֱיֵה שָׁלֵם בְּכָל נִסְיוֹנוֹתַי. See also Gen. 25:27 - וְיַעֲקֹב אִישׁ תָּם - Yaakov is called Ish Tam, Targum renders this to mean he was a גבר שלים which means 'complete.' Rashi renders Ish Tam as כְּלִבּוֹ כֵּן פִּיו - 'Whatever he was thinking, is what he said.' This matches the definition that 'Shalem and Tam mean *being complete*, so here it means Yaakov Avinu was '*completely*' congruent, his words matched his intent. When the word תמים is applied to a Korban, it means the animal is without blemish, מום. So too, The Mitzvah to be a Tam means be completely trusting in Hashem without any blemish of doubt that Hashem is perfect in His justice and all is for the good. See also Josh. 24:14 - וְעַתָּה יְראוּ אֶת־ה' וְעִבְדוּ אֹתוֹ בְּתָמִים וּבֶאֱמֶת - Yehoshua is speaking to Beney Yisrael just before he dies and he reminds us to recall Hashem's kindness to us from the time of Avraham Avinu till He took us across the Yarden, and now he instructs us to serve Hashem with Temimut and Emet. Which means to be completely filled with Emuna and trust in Hashem alone. This Mitzvah is counted by Ramban Aseh #7 and Sefer Chareidim as one of the 613 Mitzvos. It is counted as a Mitzvah performed by the Mind, or thought in the moment.

50 This is counted as one of the 613 by Ramban and Sefer Chareidim. It is derived from Num. 16:5 - לֹא יִהְיֶה כְקֹרַח וְכַעֲדָתוֹ - (Ramban Lo Taaseh #25 & Smak Mitzvah #132). Machlokes is a Mitzvah that starts in the thought of 'judging' others. It germinates as a thought that is not bridled, and before you know it, one has blown the thoughts out of proportion till one accumulates other thoughts as evidence for one's correct position against so and so. Then he is armed with all his negative and non-reality impressions of the person he differs with till he cannot control his mouth and he stirs Machloket. This Mitzvah is reminding me of the genesis of Machloket - *Thought in the moment*. If I know this is a serious Issur that can lead to self-destruction and that of one's family too (Rachmana Litzlan), one is more likely to catch one's thinking in the early stages and cut them out right there! Korach died with all his family, including sucklings and infants. He brought down 250 leaders of Beney Yisrael who also died because of his constant thoughts of jealousy which led to Machlokes. See Avot 5:17 where Chazal offer the prime example of a Machlokes not rooted in good intent (לשם שמים) is that of Korach and his followers - **כָּל מַחֲלוֹקֶת שֶׁהִיא לְשֵׁם שָׁמַיִם, סוֹפָהּ לְהִתְקַיֵּם. וְשֶׁאֵינָהּ לְשֵׁם שָׁמַיִם, אֵין סוֹפָהּ לְהִתְקַיֵּם. אֵיזוֹ הִיא מַחֲלוֹקֶת שֶׁהִיא** לְשֵׁם שָׁמַיִם, זוֹ מַחֲלוֹקֶת הִלֵּל וְשַׁמַּאי. וְשֶׁאֵינָהּ לְשֵׁם שָׁמַיִם, **זוֹ מַחֲלוֹקֶת קֹרַח וְכָל עֲדָתוֹ**:

51 Gratitude is an attitude, it is born in thought. A grateful person is thinking thoughts of appreciation. The words *Lev Tov* correctly mean a *good mind*, or *good thinking*. Now when we look at Dev. 28:47 we can better understand what this Passuk is communicating - תַּחַת אֲשֶׁר לֹא־ עָבַדְתָּ אֶת־ה' אֱלֹקֶיךָ בְּשִׂמְחָה וּבְטוּב לֵבָב מֵרֹב כֹּל - (all the frightening Tochachos and long list of retribution coming upon klal Yisrael listed before this Passuk are all because...) "...*you did not enjoy serving Hashem with good thoughts* (of gratitude) *from the abundant good* (that Hashem showers you with all the time). We were not grateful while we had it good! (Rashi there). So Simcha in the service of Hashem is directly related to our thoughts of gratitude (טוּב לֵבָב) for the abundant good in our lives (מֵרֹב כֹּל). See also Dev. 6:5 where we find the Mitzvah to love Hashem with all - בכל מאדך - all your possessions, all your assets and all your talents. Happiness and gratitude are twins. Try being happy if you are not grateful. Try being grateful without being happy. It is not possible. To be truly happy, one must have cultivated grateful thoughts for the good we are blessed with. The ultimate love of Hashem is to display our gratitude davka when

21. Zulaso-Never think there is any other power beside Hashem.⁵² NR
22. Don't have arrogant thoughts.⁵³ NR
23. Don't forget Hashem.⁵⁴ R
24. Don't complain! All complaints are really against Hashem.⁵⁵ NR
25. Be Mevater.⁵⁶ R
26. Control your thinking by ignoring negative thoughts.⁵⁷ R
27. Yiras Hashem means have no fear of anyone/anything except Hashem.⁵⁸ R

חַיָּב אָדָם לְבָרֵךְ עַל הָרָעָה כְּשֵׁם שֶׁהוּא מְבָרֵךְ עַל הַטּוֹבָה, שֶׁנֶּאֱמַר (דברים things go wrong! See Brachos 9:5 ו:ה) וְאָהַבְתָּ אֵת יְיָ אֱלֹקֶיךָ בְּכָל לְבָבְךָ וּבְכָל נַפְשְׁךָ וּבְכָל מְאֹדֶךָ....וּבְכָל מְאֹדֶךָ, בְּכָל מִדָּה וּמִדָּה דָּבָר אַחֵר בְּכָל מְאֹדֶךָ, בְּכָל מָמוֹנֶךָ. מִדָּה וּמִדָּה שֶׁהוּא מוֹדֵד לְךָ הֱוֵי מוֹדֶה לוֹ בִּמְאֹד מְאֹד. This Mishna tells us that when things go wrong and we declare our love for Hashem, we fulfil the Mitzvah to love Him. G-d can do no wrong! This Mishna's wording is Halachically quoted in Shulchan Aruch, Orach Chaim, Siman #222.3. The purpose of 100 Blessings a day is to train ourselves in reality thinking, to be grateful for our many blessings & for Hashem's constant and unlimited kindness. Birkas Hamazon has same purpose. So too Tefila of which two out of three elements are about gratitude, that is praise and thanks. Shevach V'Hodaah. R'Avigdor Miller z"l said Tov L'Hodot LaShem means this is the *only good*! To really be inspired to live a life of gratitude, we encourage you to read Rabbi Arush's best sellers 'Garden of Gratitude' and 'Garden of Miracles' which list 190 stories of people who saw open miracles in their lives directly related to their thanking Hashem especially for their suffering! You must read these two books!

52 Ex. 20:3
53 Dev. 8:17 - וְאָמַרְתָּ בִּלְבָבֶךָ כֹּחִי וְעֹצֶם יָדִי עָשָׂה לִי אֶת־הַחַיִל הַזֶּה, Smak (מצוה כב - יום א) Learns from this verse not to have thoughts of arrogance.
54 Dev. 8:11 - הִשָּׁמֶר לְךָ פֶּן־תִּשְׁכַּח אֶת־ה' אֱלֹקֶיךָ. See Ramban, Lo Taaseh #41, Smag, Dev. 6:12, 9:7, Sefer Chareidim Chapter #9, Paragraphs 6-7.
55 Sichot HaRan #38
56 Rambam includes this Midda as part of the Mitzvah of Teshuva (Hilchos Teshuva 2:10 & see Shulchan Aruch, Orach Chaim, Siman 606, S'eef #1 in the Rama). To have the Midda of a Vatran, (easy going and easily appeased and easy to forgive) is considered so worthy a character trait to deserve long life. See Megilla 28a, the extraordinary longevity of Mar Zutra was attributed to the fact that he forgave anyone who hurt him in any way and never went to sleep before forgiving them. He also attributed his long life to the fact that he was very generous with his money and not exacting on how much his family spent. כי הא - ולא עלתה על מטתי קללת חברי דמר זוטרא, כי הוה סליק לפורייה אמר: שרי ליה לכל מאן דצערן. ותתרן ממומוני הייתי - דאמר מר: איוב ותתרן בממוניה הוה, שהיה מניח פרוטה לחנוני מממוניה. See there too that Rava extolled one who has this midda of a Vatran, with the claim that one who does not look to pay back any one who hurt them, but let's go of any thoughts of revenge or resentment is paid back by Hashem by having every single one of his own deliberate Aveiros against Hashem forgiven!! The Rosh Yeshiva of Ohr Samayach, Monsey, Rabbi Yisrael Rokowsky shlita would often quote this Chazal during Neila of Yom Kippur as a 'easy pass' ticket to gain forgiveness in the last moments of Yom Kippur by truly letting go and forgiving other people's wrongs - דאמר רבא: כל המעביר על מדותיו מעבירין ממנו כל פשעיו, שנאמר (מיכה ז') נשא עון ועבר על פשע, למי נושא עון - למי שעובר על פשע. - Later on the same daf 28a, Rav Zeira attributed his longevity to the same Midda, he claimed that in his entire life he did not get upset with his family! במה שאלו תלמידיו את רבי זירא: הארכת ימים? - אמר להם: מימי לא הקפדתי בתוך ביתי. Now that is really something to aspire to!
57 Dev. 23:10 - וְנִשְׁמַרְתָּ מִכֹּל דָּבָר רָע - Which Chazal (Avoda Zara 20b) tell us means not to have Hirhurim Ra'im, bad thoughts during the day in order not to come to see Keri at night - ת"ר: (דברים כו) ונשמרת מכל דבר רע - שלא יהרהר אדם ביום ויבוא לידי טומאה בלילה. Also Num. 15:39 - Don't follow your thoughts, means any Lo Taaseh, or as we are describing - Non-Reality Thoughts.
58 Dev. 10:20 & 8:6. Yiras Hashem really means having no other fear except for losing one's relationship with G-d. Fear of Onesh, negative consequences for going against Hashem and also Awe for His greatness which is achieved through learning Torah with intent to grow in Yirat Hashem. Awe of Hashem is also achieved through the study and contemplation of His perfect

28. ובו תדבק - Constantly think of Hashem.⁵⁹   R
29. Tefila.⁶⁰   R
30. Don't think of doing Aveiros.⁶¹   R
31. Don't despair of Hashem's Rachamim.⁶²   R
32. Don't despair of Tefila to Hashem, no matter how bad the situation, instead, expect Hashem to save you.⁶³   R
33. Don't follow your negative thoughts.⁶⁴   R
34. Don't follow your eyes,⁶⁵ meaning don't trust in your mind because of what your eyes see.   R
35. Yiras Av V'Em.⁶⁶   R
36. Remember, the only cause of your success is Hashem.⁶⁷   R
37. It's a Mitzvah to think about Hashem's greatness as manifest in His creation.⁶⁸   R
38. Avoid a Safek Issur and Kal VaChomer a Vadai Issur.⁶⁹   R

Universe (Rambam, Mada, Yesodei HaTorah 2:2 - והיאך היא הדרך לאהבתו ויראתו, בשעה שיתבונן האדם במעשיו וברואיו הנפלאים הגדולים ויראה מהן חכמתו שאין לה ערך ולא קץ מיד הוא אוהב ומשבח ומפאר ומתאוה תאוה גדולה לידע השם הגדול, כמו שאמר דוד צמאה נפשי לאלקים לאל חי, וכשמחשב בדברים האלו עצמן מיד הוא נרתע לאחוריו ויפחד ויודע שהוא בריה קטנה שפלה אפלה עומדת בדעת קלה מעוטה לפני תמים דעות, כמו שאמר דוד כי אראה שמיך מעשה אצבעותיך מה אנוש כי תזכרנו, ולפי הדברים האלו אני מבאר כללים גדולים ממעשה רבון העולמים כדי שיהיו פתח למבין לאהוב את השם, כמו שאמרו חכמים בענין אהבה שמתוך כך אתה מכיר את מי שאמר והיה העולם. The purpose of such study should be for the sake of improving our love and awe for Hashem and in turn, inspire us with overwhelming gratitude for the unlimited kindness we see He does for us in His creation all because of His love for us.

59 Sefer Chareidim (Aseh #6 of Mitzvos of the Mind) counts this as a Mitzvah of the Mind and quotes Mishley 3:6 - בְּכָל־דְּרָכֶיךָ דָעֵהוּ וְהוּא יְיַשֵּׁר אֹרְחֹתֶיךָ and writes it is a Mitzvas Aseh to think about Hashem all the time. Even when eating, drinking, going to sleep, walking, going to work, and Tashmish. See Shulchan Aruch, Orach Chaim, Siman #231.

60 The essence of Tefila is Kavanat HaLev, which means 'focus of the mind,' or discipline of the mind. Tefila is a mind-set, a way of life, because one can speak to Hashem any time, any place, and ask for anything. See Rashi Ex. 17:8 (Citing Tanchuma Yisro 3 & Shir Hashirim Raba 26:2) וַיָּבֹא עֲמָלֵק וְגוֹמֵר. סָמַךְ פָּרָשָׁה זוֹ לַמִּקְרָא זֶה לוֹמַר, תָּמִיד אֲנִי בֵּינֵיכֶם וּמְזֻמָּן לְכָל צָרְכֵיכֶם, וְאַתֶּם אוֹמְרִים "הֲיֵשׁ ה' בְּקִרְבֵּנוּ אִם אָיִן"

61 Sefer Chareidim Lo Taaseh of the Mind #15 - שלא לחשוב לעשות עבירה שנאמר "ולא תתורו אחרי לבבכם"

62 Sefer Chareidim Lo Taaseh of the Mind #17 - שלא יתיאש האדם מן הרחמים - from Dev. 7:17-18

63 Sefer Chareidim Lo Taaseh of the Mind #17 - he quotes from Dev. 7:17-18 - שלא יתיאש האדם מן הרחמים ותפילה אפילו ראה אדם צרה קרובה, אלא יקוה לישועת השם שנאמר כי תאמר בלבבך רבים הגוים האלה ממני איכה אוכל להורישם: לא תירא מהם זכר תזכר את אשר־עשה ה' אלקיך לפרעה ולכל־מצרים -

64 Num. 15:39 - וְלֹא תָתוּרוּ אַחֲרֵי לְבַבְכֶם - Sefer Chareidim Lo Taaseh of the Mind #15. All Rishonim agree this is one of the 613 Mitzvos, and it is also one of the Mitzvos Tamidi, that constantly apply every second of our lives.

65 Num. 15:39 - וְלֹא תָתוּרוּ .... אַחֲרֵי עֵינֵיכֶם אֲשֶׁר־אַתֶּם זֹנִים אַחֲרֵיהֶם. Sefer Chareidim counts this as a separate Mitzvah to not following what the eyes report to one's Mind. See Brachos 9:5 where Chazal distinguish between וְלֹא תָתוּרוּ אַחֲרֵי לְבַבְכֶם to refer to forbidden thoughts of Minnus, while וְלֹא תָתוּרוּ...אַחֲרֵי עֵינֵיכֶם refers to not looking at Araiyus.

66 Lev. 19:3

67 Dev. 18:17 - See Targum there.

68 Sefer Chareidim, Aseh #15 of Mitzvos of the Mind. He derives this from Dev. 4:39 - וְיָדַעְתָּ הַיּוֹם וַהֲשֵׁבֹתָ אֶל־לְבָבֶךָ כִּי ה' הוּא הָאֱלֹקִים בַּשָּׁמַיִם מִמַּעַל וְעַל־הָאָרֶץ מִתָּחַת אֵין עוֹד. His wording there is - מצות עשה להתבונן בגדולתו יתברך. He also quotes Yishayahu 40:26 - שְׂאוּ־מָרוֹם עֵינֵיכֶם וּרְאוּ מִי־בָרָא אֵלֶּה הַמּוֹצִיא בְמִסְפָּר צְבָאָם לְכֻלָּם בְּשֵׁם יִקְרָא

39. To accept all that happens to you, your children and to your property by declaring Hashem is always right.⁷⁰   R
40. Midvar Sheker Tirchak.⁷¹   R
41. Love Hashem even when things go wrong.⁷²   R

The above list is based on the various **Rishonim** who identified these Mitzvos from Taryag which begin in **thought**. They are all Mitzvos of the Mind. Now let's see how many more are added by the same Rishonim as Mitzvos of the Mind that are Derabanan.

---

69 This Mitzvah is not counted as one of the 613 by Rambam, but Sefer Chareidim does count it (Mitzvas Aseh #13 of Mitzvos of the Mind). He derives it from the words in Dev. 30:19 - וּבָחַרְתָּ בַּחַיִּים לְמַעַן תִּחְיֶה אַתָּה וְזַרְעֶךָ.
70 Sefer Chareidim, Aseh #21 of Mitzvos of the Mind. Also the Smag in Mitzvas Aseh #17. They learn it from Dev.8:5 - וְיָדַעְתָּ עִם־לְבָבֶךָ כִּי כַּאֲשֶׁר יְיַסֵּר אִישׁ אֶת־בְּנוֹ ה' אֱלֹקֶיךָ מְיַסְּרֶךָּ. This Mitzvah is not counted by Rambam as part of Taryag, though he would agree it is still Min HaTorah.
71 Smag counts this as an Aseh (Smag Aseh #1) from Ex. 23:7 - מִדְּבַר־שֶׁקֶר תִּרְחָק - Sefer Yereim (R' Eliezer of Mitz - one of the Baaley Tosafos) in Siman #235 also counts this as one of Taryag.
72 Dev. 6:5, see Brachos 9:5.

2.8 Middos not listed in Taryag Mitzvos (Miderabanan).

The list below are many other Middos not listed in Taryag but are found in various sefarim[73] on improving middos, and *all originate in thought*!

Pay special attention to the *footnotes*. We want you to *convince yourself* of how dominant thought truly is in your life. We want you to experience how dominant Mitzvos of the Mind that Hashem instructed so many Mitzvos that directly impact thought and Middos.

The more you experience thought as the true generator of feeling and experience, the more effective you will be in implementing the strategies listed in the DVDs and later in this document.[74] All Middos are thought in the moment!

1. Make Shalom.[75] R
2. Avoid Anger.[76] NRT
3. Forgive others their wrongs against you[77] מעביר על מדותיו. R
4. Don't be disrespectful to anyone, neither an adult or child or gentile.[78] R
5. Honesty in business[79] - Emuna. R
6. Don't resist giving to a poor man charity.[80] NRT
7. Give Tzedaka with a happy face and full heartedly.[81] R
8. Be especially happy at the moment you are doing a Mitzvah.[82] R
9. Respond with silence to insults.[83] R

---

73 See Orchot Tzadikim, table of contents, Sefer Maalot HaMiddot. Messilas Yesharim, particularly Chapters #11 and #19.

74 For example, the DVDs and this document cover the Mitzvah of Tochacha as applied to the classroom. We also describe many Metaphors for teaching this great & simple lesson - *that all Middos are thought in the moment.*

75 Uktzin 3:12 - אָמַר רַבִּי שִׁמְעוֹן בֶּן חֲלַפְתָּא, לֹא מָצָא הַקָּדוֹשׁ בָּרוּךְ הוּא כְּלִי מַחֲזִיק בְּרָכָה לְיִשְׂרָאֵל אֶלָּא הַשָּׁלוֹם: שֶׁנֶּאֱמַר (תהלים כט), יְיָ עֹז לְעַמּוֹ יִתֵּן יְיָ יְבָרֵךְ אֶת עַמּוֹ בַשָּׁלוֹם. See also Avot 1:12 Where Hillel instructs us to emulate the students of Aron who were - אוהב שלום ורודף שלום.

76 Sefer Chareidim counts this in Mitzvos done with the Mind, Lo Taaseh #4, quoting Tehilim 81:10 - לֹא־יִהְיֶה בְךָ אֵל זָר and quotes Shabbos 104a that anger is equivalent to Avoda Zara. He also quotes the Zohar who equates not to make a metal sculpture for oneself (Ex. 34:17) with not becoming angry. Anger uproots the Neshama Hass Veshalom and replaces it with a Ruach Tumah.

77 Megilla 28a

78 Avot. 1:12 and 4:3. Also see Shaarei Kedusha, Rabbi Chaim Vital z"l, Chelek Aleph, Shaar Gimel where he writes in the context of purifying ones Middos, that one should love all of Hashem's creations, including gentiles - יאהב את כל הבריות אפילו גוים.

79 Shabbos 31a.

80 Dev. 15:10

81 Sefer Chareidim.

82 See Orchot Tzadikim, Shaar HaSimcha where he says a Mitzvah done with Simcha is worth a thousand times more than a Mitzvah without Simcha. Sefer Chareidim Mitzvas Aseh Derabanan of the Mind #4, he derives it from Tehilim 100:2 - עִבְדוּ אֶת־ה' בְּשִׂמְחָה.

83 Brachos 17a, Shulchan Aruch, Orach Chaim, 122:1, and incorporated into the end of Shemoneh Esrei - ולמקללי מרמה מדבר ושפתותי מרע לשוני נצור אלקי, הכי אמר צלותיה מסיים הוה כי דרבינא בריה מר נפשי תדום ונפשי כעפר לכל תהיה.

10. Midda of Silence.[84]   R
11. Don't be ungrateful, a Koffer Tov.[85]   NRT
12. Don't have Azus, impudence, or be obstinate.[86]   NRT
13. Avoid worry,[87] anxiety.[88]   NRT
14. Have Zerizus,[89] enthusiasm, especially when doing Mitzvos.   R
15. Don't be Lazy.[90]   NRT
16. Flattery.[91]   NRT

---

[84] Lev. 10:9

[85] Avoda Zara 5a at the bottom of the daf, quoting Dev. 5:26 - מִי־יִתֵּן וְהָיָה לְבָבָם זֶה לָהֶם לְיִרְאָה אֹתִי וְלִשְׁמֹר אֶת־כָּל־מִצְוֹתַי כָּל־הַיָּמִים לְמַעַן יִיטַב לָהֶם וְלִבְנֵיהֶם לְעֹלָם - Which Chazal explain we were ungrateful to Hashem. The Gemora says being an ingrate began with Adam HaRishon for being ungrateful to Hashem when instead of admitting his mistake blamed his wife whom Hashem gifted to him for eating from the tree!

תנו רבנן: (דברים ה:כו) מי יתן והיה לבבם זה להם - אמר להן משה לישראל: **כפויי טובה בני כפויי טובה**, בשעה שאמר הקדוש ברוך הוא לישראל: מי יתן והיה לבבם זה להם, היה להם לומר: תן אתה. **כפויי טובה**, דכתיב: (במדבר כא) "ונפשנו קצה בלחם הקלוקל" **בני כפויי טובה**, דכתיב: (בראשית ג) האשה אשר נתתה עמדי היא נתנה לי מן העץ ואכל.

[86] Avot. 5:20. עַז פָּנִים לְגֵיהִנָּם.

[87] There are two types of worry or anxiety. Either *thought* about the *past* or *thought* about the *future*. Anxiety for past events is a pure waste of thinking, because the past is history and is no longer here! As Chazal put it (Yuma 9a) מה דהוה הוה - 'What happened - happened!' The second type of worry, is anxiety about the future. This is even more futile, as Chazal explain (Sanhedrin 100b) *'Don't suffer tomorrow today*! Tomorrow will for sure arrive but you might not be alive to see it! So you will have suffered today for nothing! That same time I was suffering in my mind over the future, I lost out on living in today! The only time I actually live in! Here is the lashon of Chazal there in Sanhedrin 100b - שמא (משלי כ"ז:א) כי לא תלד מה ילד יום, **אל תצר צרת מחר** למחר אינונו, ונמצא מצטער על עולם שאינו שלו. Shlomo HaMelech is warning me not to spend thought over a world I cannot see (tomorrow) because tomorrow may indeed arrive but I might not be alive to see it! See Rashi there who writes - **מה ילד יום** - מה אירע היום, שמא למחר אינונו - שמת הוא. ונמצא - שמיצער על יום שאינו עתיד לראותו, והייונ עולם שלו שהוא שאינו נתתה עליו, ודואג על חנם מיום המחרת שלא תבא עליו צרה.

[88] Sanhedrin 100b - 'Don't let thoughts of worry enter your mind, for many extremely strong men have been killed by worry!' לא תעיל דויא בלבך דגברי גיברין קטל דויא. The same Gemora then tells us what to do if we have unrelenting thoughts of worry or anxiety - quoting Shlomo HaMelech - משלי י"ב:כה **דאגה בלב איש ישחנה**. רבי אמי ורבי אסי, חד אמר: **ישחנה מדעתו**, וחד אמר: **ישיחנה - לאחרים**. See Yuma 7a explaining this Passuk in Mishley. The point being, plan A is Don't have thoughts of worry. Plan B is if you do have such pop-thoughts, then delete them, meaning שיחנה מדעתו, take your mind off such thoughts. Plan C is that if the first two plans did not work, the thoughts of anxiety and worry keep returning, then speak to others. The Gemora does not give instructions to the 'others' who are listening to him, it just says he should 'speak to others.' The implication being solution C is in his speaking about what is on his mind and others listening. That is all he really needs. From the position of the listeners, they however should encourage him to go back to plan A and divert his thoughts away from thoughts of anxiety and worry. The most powerful way to do that is to recognize that your thoughts are simply thought! As soon as they appear, they are gone, forever, never to return. If the thought does come back, it is a brand new thought! Because you only live in the now, the previous thought is part of history, dead, no longer here!

[89] Avot. 5:20. הֱוֵי עַז כַּנָּמֵר, וְקַל כַּנֶּשֶׁר, וְרָץ כַּצְּבִי, וְגִבּוֹר כָּאֲרִי לַעֲשׂוֹת רְצוֹן אָבִיךָ שֶׁבַּשָּׁמָיִם. See Yehoshua 1:6-9 - **חֲזַק וֶאֱמָץ** ז **רַק חֲזַק וֶאֱמַץ מְאֹד** לִשְׁמֹר לַעֲשׂוֹת כְּכָל־הַתּוֹרָה אֲשֶׁר צִוְּךָ מֹשֶׁה עַבְדִּי אַל־תָּסוּר מִמֶּנּוּ יָמִין וּשְׂמֹאול לְמַעַן תַּשְׂכִּיל בְּכֹל אֲשֶׁר תֵּלֵךְ: ט **הֲלוֹא צִוִּיתִיךָ חֲזַק וֶאֱמָץ אַל־תַּעֲרֹץ וְאַל־תֵּחָת כִּי עִמְּךָ ה' אֱלֹקֶיךָ בְּכֹל אֲשֶׁר תֵּלֵךְ**: You see from these verses of encouragement to Yehoshua directly from Hashem Himself. They are quoted in Messilat Yesharim chapter 6 where he defines the Midda of Zerizut. See the entire Chapter there as well as Chapters 7 - 9.

[90] Mishley 6:10-11. See Ramchal in Messilat Yesharim, Chapter 6 where he explains the Midda of Laziness in more detail.

17. Resilience.⁹²   R
18. Solution conscious (looking for Nekudos Tovos).⁹³   R
19. Don't think about Avoda Zara.⁹⁴   NRT
20. Recognize your true Self-esteem - Tzelem Elokim.⁹⁵   R
21. Nedivat Halev - be generous.⁹⁶   R
22. Humility.⁹⁷   R
23. Tzniut.⁹⁸   R
24. Boosha.⁹⁹   R

---

91 See Mishley 17:15 - מַצְדִּיק רָשָׁע וּמַרְשִׁיעַ צַדִּיק תּוֹעֲבַת יְהֹוָה גַּם־שְׁנֵיהֶם, see Rabeinu Yona there who explains this warning refers to flattery. See also שער החנופה in Orchot Tzadikim. The bottom line is that flattery has to do with saying one thing and *thinking* another. This evil Midda was the way Lavan and Esav operated. Esav is described as וַיְהִי עֵשָׂו אִישׁ יֹדֵעַ צַיִד אִישׁ שָׂדֶה וְיַעֲקֹב אִישׁ תָּם יֹשֵׁב אֹהָלִים. The Torah defines Esav as someone who traps with the mouth. Rashi quotes Chazal that he trapped his father with his mouth, pretending to be frum but really uninterested in Yiddishkeit! Esav said one thing but had in mind another, he was two faced. Unlike Yaakov who the Torah defined as an **אִישׁ תָּם** וְיַעֲקֹב which Rashi renders as someone who you could rely on whatever he said was a perfect reflection of what he thought - **כלבו כן פיו**. Here is the full description of Rashi on the two brothers - וַיִּגְדְּלוּ הַנְּעָרִים וַיְהִי עֵשָׂו. כָּל זְמַן שֶׁהָיוּ קְטַנִּים לֹא הָיוּ נִכָּרִים בְּמַעֲשֵׂיהֶם וְאֵין אָדָם מְדַקְדֵּק בָּהֶם מַה טִּיבָם, כֵּיוָן שֶׁנַּעֲשׂוּ בְּנֵי שְׁלֹשׁ עֶשְׂרֵה שָׁנָה, זֶה פֵּרַשׁ לְבָתֵּי מִדְרָשׁוֹת וְזֶה פֵּרַשׁ לַעֲבוֹדַת אֱלִילִים (ב"ר סג:י): יֹדֵעַ צָיִד. לָצוּד וּלְרַמּוֹת אֶת אָבִיו בְּפִיו, וְשׁוֹאֲלוֹ, אַבָּא, הֵיאַךְ מְעַשְּׂרִין אֶת הַמֶּלַח וְאֶת הַתֶּבֶן, כְּסָבוּר אָבִיו שֶׁהוּא מְדַקְדֵּק בְּמִצְוֹת (שם): אִישׁ שָׂדֶה. כְּמַשְׁמָעוֹ, אָדָם בָּטֵל, וְצוֹדֶה בְקַשְׁתּוֹ חַיּוֹת וְעוֹפוֹת: תָּם. אֵינוֹ בָקִי בְּכָל אֵלֶּה, כְּלִבּוֹ כֵּן פִּיו. מִי שֶׁאֵינוֹ חָרִיף לְרַמּוֹת קָרוּי "תָּם":

92 Avot. 5:3 Avraham Avinu was tested ten times by Hashem and he stood up to every test. The language of standing is 'resilience.' Never giving up. Never despair. Start again, no matter how many times you fall. This was the Midda of Avraham Avinu. See Rashi and Rabeinu Yona on that Mishna, Avot 5:3 who define 'standing' as not thinking about the Nissayon! He just did what he was told without second guessing Hashem's intent. See also Chidushei HaRim on Shabbos 92a, of the 4 qualities needed for Hashem to rest his Shechina on a person, the last one is a בעל קומה, someone who is tall. Or literally 'a master of standing.' Says the Chiddushei HaRim, it means someone who is so resilient that no matter how many times he falls, he **stands up** and starts again!

93 Likutei Moharan, I, Lesson 282. The very word שטן are the Rashei Tovos נקודות טובות שונא (Rabbi Shalom Arush shlita).

94 Lev. 19:4

95 Lev. 19:18, deduced from the word כמוך in the verse **וְאָהַבְתָּ לְרֵעֲךָ כָּמוֹךָ** - the predicate in the passuk is that I love myself!

96 Ex. 25:2, see Rashi.

97 Num. 12:3.

98 Micha 6:8 - הִגִּיד לְךָ אָדָם מַה־טּוֹב וּמָה־ה' דּוֹרֵשׁ מִמְּךָ כִּי אִם־עֲשׂוֹת מִשְׁפָּט וְאַהֲבַת חֶסֶד **וְהַצְנֵעַ לֶכֶת עִם־אֱלֹהֶיךָ**. See Radak there who explains that the command to be 'Tzanua walking with Hashem' refers to 'total love for Hashem.' The Navi writes the words **הַצְנֵעַ לֶכֶת עִם־אֱלֹהֶיךָ** to denote instructions for the mind which is hidden, Tzanua, concealed. See Rashi on Ex.34:3 - (תנחומא אֵין לְךָ יָפֶה מִן הַצְּנִיעוּת לֹא)

99 Avot. 5:20 וּבֹשֶׁת פָּנִים לְגַן עֵדֶן. Boosha is loosely translates as 'shame.' It refers to natural shame that comes from recognizing one's own lowly self, relative to Hashem's greatness. The greater a person or Tzadik, the more shame they feel in the Presence of Hashem. It is a form of embarrassment for one's violations against The King of Kings. One could illustrate this with a simple metaphor of the shame felt by a subject after realizing he misbehaved in front of the King who gives him all his sustenance, he feels so so ashamed for being so ungrateful and thus disloyal that he does not know where to put himself. Shaul HaMelech had such Boosha. Boosha is thought, because it is knowing in one's mind that one is nothing and a nobody in light of Hashem's unlimited kindness.

3.0 The Mitzvah of Tochacha

When a Jew is upset with another Jew, we have a healing Mitzvah of Tochacha to bring them back into rapport. This Mitzvah of Tochacha is not the first option though. It comes after the Mitzvah not to Think![100]

3.1 How Does Hashem want me to respond to hardships in life?[101]

There are three levels of how Hashem wants us to *think* when something does not go our way in a relationship, friendship, marriage, learning partner, school friend, roommate, co-worker, boss, client, etc.

These three levels of response to adversity are what we are role modeling for our children!
1. Don't think about it! Instead declare your love for Hashem!
2. Judging others is not my business!
3. The Mitzvah of Tochacha

We will now explain each of these.

---

[100] The Mitzvah 'not to think' means not to let thoughts of doubting Hashem's perfect justice enter our mind. If doubts do enter, 'press delete' by not thinking it in the next thought! The Torah itself testifies that the purpose of Hashem showing His constant kindness upon us is to test our thoughts! Will we be grateful or complain? Will we continue to love and keep His Mitzvos or will we doubt His Presence? This is demonstrated in Ex.17:7-8 when we were tested by Hashem with a three-day lack of water, instead of our asking Moshe Rabeinu to ask Hashem for His Rachamim and give us water, we complained and even questioned whether Hashem's Presence is still with us! - וַיִּקְרָא שֵׁם הַמָּקוֹם מַסָּה וּמְרִיבָה עַל־רִיב בְּנֵי יִשְׂרָאֵל וְעַל נַסֹּתָם אֶת־ה' לֵאמֹר הֲיֵשׁ ה' בְּקִרְבֵּנוּ אִם־אָיִן. The response is in the subsequent verse describing Amalek's attack upon us - וַיָּבֹא עֲמָלֵק וַיִּלָּחֶם עִם־יִשְׂרָאֵל בִּרְפִידִם Our mistake was to question altogether whether Hashem is still with us! That is unthinkable! We should never allow such thoughts to fester. If they pop up, let go and be מסיח דעת in the next thought. If you have trouble letting go of such pop-up thoughts, then turn your next moment (thought) into a Tefila and Praise Hashem Who gives you the Yetzer Hara because He knows you can ignore it and ask Hashem to help you let go of such thoughts. See also Rashi on Dev. 8:2 where Moshe Rabeynu reminds us to not to have thoughts of doubt against Hashem - וְזָכַרְתָּ אֶת־כָּל־הַדֶּרֶךְ אֲשֶׁר הוֹלִיכֲךָ ה' אֱלֹקֶיךָ זֶה אַרְבָּעִים שָׁנָה בַּמִּדְבָּר לְמַעַן עַנֹּתְךָ לְנַסֹּתְךָ **לָדַעַת** **אֶת־אֲשֶׁר בִּלְבָבְךָ** הֲתִשְׁמֹר מִצְוֹתָיו אִם־לֹא and Rashi there who tells us that after all the 40 year trek of continuous kindness, we are being tested by Hashem to how we respond to the times when it was not easy, will we still be grateful or will we doubt His continuous kindness to us? - שֶׁלֹּא **תְנַסֵּהוּ וְלֹא תְהַרְהֵר אַחֲרָיו**. The bottom line here is that *whatever happens to us, is really Hashem showing up in our lives masked behind people and events*. All His showing up is one continuous test. And what is that test? Will we judge Hashem or fall into the trap of judging the people Hashem sends to test our internal resilience?

[101] Please note that in the accompanying DVD, 3.1 goes straight into the 3 steps of the Tochacha Formula. In this document, we are giving more Hashkafa behind this formula, so the numbering is slightly different. The 3 steps in the Tochacha Formula are in 3.5 in this document.

3.2 Plan 'A' is The Mitzvah 'Not to Think' - But 'Thank' Instead![102]

Plan A of how to respond to people who upset us is '*Forgive & Forget!*' In other words, 'let go!" Be Mevater.' *Stop thinking* about what so and so did to you!

Plan A is the Midda to let go and forgive as Chazal describe - **המעביר על מדותיו**,[103] When we forgive, we are forgiven.[104]

To be **מוחל** literally means to 'erase' as in 'erase the memory of their mistakes done to you' [105]
The full Mitzvah of forgiveness, 'to erase what they did,' means *don't even remember their faults* (Netira).[106]

How do I just let go of my resentment toward others who hurt me?

Chazal encourage us to fulfil the Mitzvah of Ahavas Hashem when we experience other people's negativity! How? By saying 'thank You to Hashem.'

The last Mishna in Brachos tells us the meaning of loving Hashem with all your **מאודך** - means to be exceedingly, exceedingly grateful when bad things happen to us!

חַיָּב אָדָם לְבָרֵךְ עַל הָרָעָה כְּשֵׁם שֶׁהוּא מְבָרֵךְ עַל הַטּוֹבָה, שֶׁנֶּאֱמַר (דברים ו:ה) וְאָהַבְתָּ אֵת יְיָ אֱלֹקֶיךָ בְּכָל לְבָבְךָ וּבְכָל נַפְשְׁךָ וּבְכָל מְאֹדֶךָ. בְּכָל לְבָבְךָ, בִּשְׁנֵי יְצָרֶיךָ, בְּיֵצֶר טוֹב

---

102 Please note, 3.2 in the DVD defines who the Rebbe/Morah is and is not. In this document, that appears in 3.6.
103 Yuma 23a - כל המעביר על מדותיו - מעבירין לו על כל פשעיו
104 Actually, Chazal tell us we get a bonus forgiveness when forgiving others because we are forgiven for deliberate sins against Hashem - מעבירין לו על כל פשעיו.
105 מוחל is from the three letter root מחה - erase. See Rambam, Deos, 6:9 where he rules that the best way for a person to respond to insult or hurt is forgive him and not conceal any thoughts/feelings of hatred. Either because he realizes the person was simply a fool and to speak to him about it will not help anyway, or because the person said or did what he did out of confusion but not ill intent. Forgiving him and not even talking to him about it is the Midda of Hassidus. Here are Rambam's words - מי שחטא עליו חבירו ולא רצה להוכיחו ולא לדבר לו כלום מפני שהיה החוטא הדיוט ביותר, או שהיתה דעתו משובשת, **ומחל לו בלבו** ולא שטמו ולא הוכיחו הרי זו מדת חסידות. See also Rambam, Deos, 6:6. where he gives you the third option of Tochacha - כשיחטא איש לאיש לא ישטמנו וישתוק אלא מצוה עליו להודיעו ולומר לו למה עשית לי כך וכך ולמה חטאת לי בדבר פלוני, שנאמר הוכח תוכיח את עמיתך, **ואם חזר ובקש ממנו למחול לו צריך למחול**, ולא יהא המוחל אכזרי שנאמר ויתפלל אברהם אל האלקים.
106 Yuma 23a. Rashi there explaining what it means not to hold a grudge - Netira - **איני כמותך שלא השאלתני זו היא נטירה - שהדבר שמור בלבו, ולא הסיח מדעתו**. Meaning, the memory of my neighbor's refusal to lend me his tool is being 'guarded' in my mind and I am refusing to let go of this thought/memory. Only Hashem Who designed us can tell us what we can do, and He is encouraging us, instructing us, to believe we are able to let go of resentment. Otherwise He could not command us not to think such thoughts!

וּבְיֵצֶר רָע. וּבְכָל נַפְשְׁךָ, אֲפִלּוּ הוּא נוֹטֵל אֶת נַפְשֶׁךָ. וּבְכָל מְאֹדֶךָ, בְּכָל מָמוֹנֶךָ. דָּבָר אַחֵר בְּכָל מְאֹדֶךָ, בְּכָל מִדָּה וּמִדָּה שֶׁהוּא מוֹדֵד לְךָ הֱוֵי מוֹדֶה לוֹ בִּמְאֹד מְאֹד

This Mishna is quoted as the definitive Halacha in Shulchan Aruch: **Orach Chaim, Siman #222:3**
חייב אדם לברך על הרע בדעת שלימה ובנפש חפצה כדרך שמברך בשמחה על הטובה. כי הרעה לעובדי השם היא שמחתם וטובתם, כיון שמקבל מאהבה מה שגזר עליו השם - נמצא שבקבלת רעה זו - הוא עובד השם שהיא שמחה לו.

This Halacha is not described as only applying to Tzadikim, but to each and every one of us! The wording is חייב אדם! Every person!

This is not a one-time choice, it is a lifetime career in being happy even when things do not go right.

This is the highest level of dealing with differences.

This level may be easier for some people because their nature is to be extremely easy going, but for most of us mortals, it is a lot of hard work to remember Hashem is inviting us to love Him when He sends difficult and different people in our faces!

It is hard work to remind ourselves of Hashem's reality! But that is the whole point, Hashem's reality is what we are aiming to emulate and He literally hides behind the small and big obstacles in our lives, waiting for us to find Him there![107]

Hashem's reality is His Mitzvos of the mind! In the domain of thought, each one of us has our own reality. Hashem asks me for my *silence* or my being *mevater* or my even being *happy* when He sends me difficult people.[108]

If I cannot be silent, or mevater, or happy with people who are hurting me, if I cannot help judging others, then I have the Mitzvah of Tochacha!

Tochacha is level number three of how to respond to upset. The first two levels are synonymous with our thrice daily request ולמקללי נפשי תדום and ונפשי כעפר לכל תהיה. Let's look at **Plan B** or level two of responding to upset.

---

[107] See Likutei Moharan I. Torah #115.
[108] See Shulchan Aruch, Orach Chaim, #222.3

3.3 Plan B - Judging Others is Not My Business!

This has three levels in Chazal:

1. G-d did not appoint me to be His policeman![109] - אל תהי דן יחידי שאין דן יחידי אלא אחד

2. When you are in his shoes, then you can pass judgement![110]
אל תדין את חברך עד שתגיע למקומו
Who in all history shared the same place as another human, same background, same experiences, same education, same opportunities, same mind and thoughts?? Nobody, it never happened or ever will! So, Chazal are really saying never judge anybody! You just never really know their story, and does not everyone have their unique story!?

3. If I cannot resist judging, then I have to select a favorable interpretation of their behavior![111]
הוי דן את כל האדם לכף זכות

If 'Not Thinking' and 'Not Judging' Fails then Go To Plan C - Give Tochacha. Let's look at the rules of Tochacha:

---

109 Avot 4:8. Rebi Yishmael, the son of Rebi Yossi says - אַל תְּהִי דָן יְחִידִי, שֶׁאֵין דָּן יְחִידִי אֶלָּא אֶחָד
110 Avot. 2:4. Hillel says - וְאַל תָּדִין אֶת חֲבֵרְךָ עַד שֶׁתַּגִּיעַ לִמְקוֹמוֹ
111 Avot. 1:6. Yehoshua Ben Perachia - וֶהֱוֵי דָן אֶת כָּל הָאָדָם לְכַף זְכוּת

3.4 Plan C. Give Tochacha. Here are the Rules - Hilchos Tochacha.

Rambam[112] defines the Mitzvah of Tochacha as 'clarification.' Not an accusation or statement predicated on knowing you wronged me.

He offers two scripts for the Mitzvah of Tochacha, both scripts are in question format to give his friend a chance to explain or apologize:

1. למה עשיתה כך וכך ?
2. למה חטאת לי בדבר פלוני ?[113]

The 6 conditions Rambam gives in this Mitzvah:

1. **Privately**[114] and not in front of anyone else.
2. **Pleasantly** - וידבר לו בנחת
3. **Soft voice**[115] - ובלשון רכות
4. **Let him know you** are saying this for A. **His benefit** - ויודיע לו שאינו אומר לו אלא לטובתו and B. **To bring him to** הבא העולם חיי
5. If one cannot speak except with anger[116], or raised voice then it is better to **say nothing**.
6. Don't speak in a way that might **embarrass or humiliate**.[117] That is itself an Aveira from the Torah and is written immediately next to the words of the Mitzvah to give Tochacha in order to tell me that giving Tochacha is conditional on not humiliating the person.

---

112 Deos 6:6-9.
113 Note the language is **למה** and not **מדוע**. Rambam is quoting the lashon of Chazal (Sifri in B'ha'alosecha 12:9 and Erchin16b) with the implication that the direction of the question is more about how to move forward than analyzing the past. If you want to extrapolate the difference between the two 'whys' - **מדוע** and **למה**, the word **מדוע** would be a 'why' question about the past, requesting 'why did it come to this' and that might open up an entire can of worms with digging and analyzing the past. **למה** is a very different 'why.' It correctly translates as '*for what*' or '*to what....*' for what reason or purpose or benefit?' It sends us into the future. The focus is thus on how can we resolve this moving forward rather than analyzing the past and passing judgement.
114 Deos. 6:7 - המוכיח את חבירו בין בדברים שבינו לבינו, בין בדברים שבינו לבין המקום, צריך להוכיחו בינו לבין עצמו, וידבר לו בנחת ובלשון רכה ויודיעו שאינו אומר לו אלא לטובתו להביאו לחיי העולם הבא
115 Rambam, Deos 6:7. See Shabbos 34a and Gittin 6b.
116 Rambam Deos 6:7 - "וידבר לו בנחת ובלשון רכה...". See also Yalkut Shimoni on Tehilim 6:2 where he quotes Keneset Yisrael as praying to Hashem not to give us Tochacha from anger.
117 Rambam Deos 6:8 - המוכיח את חבירו תחלה לא ידבר לו קשות עד שיכלימנו שנאמר ולא תשא עליו חטא, כך אמרו חכמים יכול אתה מוכיחו ופניו משתנות ת"ל ולא תשא עליו חטא, **מכאן שאסור לאדם להכלים את ישראל** וכל שכן ברבים, אע"פ שהמכלים את חבירו אינו לוקה עליו עון גדול הוא, כך אמרו חכמים המלבין פני חבירו ברבים אין לו חלק לעולם הבא, לפיכך צריך אדם להזהר שלא לבייש חבירו ברבים בין קטן בין גדול, ולא יקרא לו בשם שהוא בוש ממנו, ולא יספר לפניו דבר שהוא בוש ממנו

Chazal expressed surprise that anyone could give Tochacha correctly or even be Mekabel Tochacha![118] - א"ר טרפון: תמה אני אם יש בדור הזה שמקבל תוכחה, אם אמר לו טול קיסם מבין עיניך, אמר לו טול קורה מבין עיניך. אמר רבי אלעזר בן עזריה: תמיהני אם יש בדור הזה שיודע להוכיח

When it is clear that Tochacha will not be accepted, the Mitzvah does not apply.[119] It is best to be silent.[120]
Tochacha does not mean to "tell off" or "rebuke" or "reprimand." All those are translations that do not reflect the meaning or intent in Lashon HaKodesh. The word 'תוכחה' explains Rashi, means בירור דברים,[121] 'clarification.' To clarify means to 'bring to light' and 'prove clearly.' This meaning gives this Mitzvah a very different sounding than the translation of 'reprimand' or 'tell off' or 'rebuke,' all of which imply upset, disappointment or even outrage and anger. Yet, as we saw, once anger is in the mix, the Mitzvah of Tochacha falls away.

The Rebbe and Morah have signed up for a real crash course in Middos! To hold *ourselves* to the standard of not being angry with a student when attempting to 'discipline' them.

---

118 Erchin 16b
119 Shulchan Aruch, Orach Chayim, Biur Halacha in סימן תרח - ד"ה "אבל". The Biur Halacha also quotes the Gra who claims that Tosafot (Shabbos 55 - ד"ה אע"ג) is lenient not to give Tochacha to the Tzibur where it is clear they will not listen. The Gra agrees with the opinion of the Smag in Aseh #11 where the Smag concludes that even for people who are doing Aveiros B'Meizid, it is best to remain silent where it is clear they would not listen. He quotes the Gemora in Yevamos 65 - חייב אדם שלא לומר דבר שלא נשמע שנאמר "לא תוכח לץ שמא ישנאך". See also Likutei Moharan II. Torah 8.1 where Reb Nachman of Breslov explains how Rebi Eliezer Ben Azaria's opinion applies even more so nowadays, that there is nobody who can give Tochacha without causing more damage than correction.
120 Smag, Aseh, #11 at the end.
121 Rashi on Gen. 24:44 - הוכיח בָּרַר וְהוֹדִיעַ, וְכֵן כָּל הוֹכָחָה שֶׁבַּמִּקְרָא בֵּרוּר דָּבָר. See also Rashi on Gen. 24:14 - בֵּרַרְתָּ 'הוֹכַחְתָּ' אַפְרוֹבִיש"ט (הברהת) בְּלַע"ז: . 'you have clarified' or in old French Aprover which means 'to prove.'

3.5 Practical Applications of Tochacha

The Tochacha Formula - 3 Steps! That's all!
This is the formula for Tochacha we will explore three simple steps:

1. Collect information - "What happened?" - Who claims what!
2. Ask "did you do the right thing to...."
3. Ask "what should you do?" (apologize)

There is a 'Step 4' which is a 'Reflective Step' to help the student explore how else he could have handled the conflict instead of what he did. We will explore this after we have looked at a role play of the first three crucial steps of Tochacha.

3.6 Dear Rebbe/Morah! Who Are you and Who Are You not?

In my role as 'Rebbe/Morah' Am I also Policeman, Judge, or Arbitrator?

In all the following scenarios, it is really vital the teacher remain with an 'asking' voice and not an 'accusative' tone.

The teacher is not the class police man, judge or arbitrator, the teacher helps the children in the Mitzvah of Tochacha by role modeling for them how to search for clarity (remember Tochacha means a search for clarity - בירור דברים) and make Shalom.

The student will be able to detect in your voice if you are accusative or helping them untangle their own conflicts. Your facial expression, tone of voice and choice of words will reveal if you are taking the role of class Policeman/judge/arbitrator (this is the Middos work for the teacher!) or sincerely helping them become their own solvers of conflict.

3.7 Sample Scenario - Role Model Tochacha.[122]

It is quite ironic that we know exactly what to do when a child does not understand math addition, we show him how to add.
- If he does not know how to subtract, multiply or divide, we show him how to subtract, multiply and divide.
- If he does not know how to remember the names of the parts of the human anatomy, we teach him ways to remember.
- If he does not know how to read, we teach him how to read.
- If he does not know how to behave, we *punish* him!! Hhhm! Strange! Why don't we *show* him how to behave?

Why is there an assumption that I can skip *role modeling how to behave* and shoot for a punishment before I have ascertained if the student has been shown how to behave!?

The Torah gives me a way to resolve conflict - The Mitzvah of Tochacha.

This Mitzvah is literally the bridge between hate and love.

The Mitzvah not to hate another Jew is Lev. 19:17 - לֹא־תִשְׂנָא אֶת־אָחִיךָ בִּלְבָבֶךָ and the Mitzvah to love another Jew *is only one verse later*, Lev. 19:18 - וְאָהַבְתָּ לְרֵעֲךָ כָּמוֹךָ !
How am I supposed to go from *hatred* to *love* so quickly?

Look closer and you will see there is another Mitzvah in between them, the Mitzvah of Tochacha - הוֹכֵחַ תּוֹכִיחַ אֶת־עֲמִיתֶךָ. This Mitzvah, when done correctly, *turns hatred into love*. Tochacha is the Bridge to cross over from Hate to Love.[123] It's the Healing Mitzvah!

Step 1 - Collect Information from Reuven & Shimon.

Reuven comes to you crying, he says Shimon hurt him.
Teacher to Reuven: *"What did Shimon do to you?"*
Reuven answers: *"Shimon said I am dumb"*
Teacher to Reuven: *"Did you ask Shimon why he said that?"*
Encourage Reuven to ask Shimon why Shimon called him dumb. If Reuven refuses or is too emotional to talk, then Teacher asks Shimon.

Teacher: *"Shimon! do you know why Reuven is crying?"*

---

[122] Please note that in the DVD version this section **Sample Scenario - Role Model Tochacha** appears as 3.3.
[123] I heard this insight from Rabbi Yaakov Greenwald z"l, who heard it from the Steipler Gaon z"l.

Shimon might shrug his shoulders as though to say "how do I know? And I don't care!"

Is it is true you called Shimon "dumb."
Reuven answers: "*Well yes I did but that's because Shimon tore my picture.*"
This step is called 'collecting information.' You, the teacher (parent) have heard two generations of accusations. Generation #1 when Shimon called Reuven 'dumb.' As you collected information from Shimon, you discovered the *previous generation* of accusation which led Shimon to call Reuven 'dumb,' which was because Shimon had torn Reuven's picture. The tearing of Reuven's paper is Generation #2.

Do not explore more than two generations of accusations!

You do not want to get caught in a spiral of earlier generations of accusations, meaning - Shimon claims he tore Reuven's paper because Reuven would not let Shimon play on his team in recess. 'Not letting him play in recess' would count as a third generation of accusation.

There is a deeper meaning to this: Once a teacher falls into the trap of asking for more than two generations of accusations, he is no longer role playing for the children how to resolve differences by themselves. Instead the teacher has jumped into a role of 'Policeman Rebbe' or 'Policewoman Morah,' or 'Classroom Judge' and 'Arbitrator.'
You are not here to find out the truth!
You are not here to adjudicate justice in the classroom!
If you do fall into the trap of judging, then you have -
- Taught the children to come to you for every arbitration.
- Taught the children they cannot be relied upon to resolve their own conflicts, they are disempowered!
- We actually perpetuate the problem of the children not learning to deal with conflicts!
- We teach them to persuade higher authorities to rule in favor of their behavior.

Falling into the trap of 'policeman Rebbe' means -
1. The child falls into a trap of being a victim or target and the 'other' kid is the 'bad' boy or 'bully' of the class.
2. This feeds a culture in the classroom of whoever is better at persuading rebbe of the severity of the crime committed against him by his peers - *wins*, and whoever is punished is the *loser*.
3. We have a pattern of winners and losers, at least one child will walk away feeling he was dealt with unjustly.
4. They often lose trust in the teacher (and possibly adults altogether).
5. They build up resentment and anger which could have been totally avoided.
6. Children learn they have to be street smart to manipulate others to avoid getting hurt or caught.
7. They learn that this class is not safe and my teacher does not protect me.

Too many mistaken and confusing messages are taught when we think our job is to arbitrate between who is right and who is wrong.

This simple method of role modeling Tochacha is about guiding the children to figure out the solutions *themselves* without getting entangled in multi-generational accusations.
The Mitzvah of Tochacha is about staying focused on their **response to conflict** and **not** *who is to blame* or *how severe was the crime* and now *how they get justice* meted out.

Falling into the trap of class 'policeman' means you will never know the real truth behind the accusations unless you are a witness in Beis Din with another witness who gives the identical testimony and a Beis Din of qualified judges give their verdict. But that is not what the classroom is meant to be.

You are not a dayan on Beis Din. You are their adult guardian, entrusted to teach Torah and in the arena of Middos, you are their role model of how to deal with conflict. Now let's go to the next step.

According to Rav Moshe Feinstein z"l, *unless a teacher actually witnessed what the student did wrong, he is not allowed to punish him. Only two adult witnesses can testify against a wrongdoing in front of Bais Din (but the testimony of another child against a peer is not sufficient to permit a teacher to hit or punish). A teacher is not allowed to punish a student based on suspicion, even if the rebbe thinks this student has a track record of misbehavior. Even if all* conditions are fulfilled, that is, he knows with absolute certainty this student did wrong, the teacher can only give a punishment if he has Yishuv HaDaas but not with anger or rage. It is despicable for a rebbe to ask the class to tell on another student as this undermines the severity of Lashon Hara.[124]

Step 2a - Ask Shimon did he do the right thing to...

In this step, the teacher only focuses on asking questions. Ask questions which direct the child to his own internal compass. They already know the answers, you are just helping them find the answers inside themselves. The assumption you operate from is *your trust in their ability to resolve the conflict*.

Your tone of voice here plays a crucial role. If you sound accusative, you will be seen as taking sides, they will defend themselves instead of wanting to cooperate with this formula for Tochacha.

If your tone is gentle, pleasant, and simply inquisitive, you will be seen as sincerely looking to help the children without discipline or punishment or taking sides.

Your gentle tone will also help both of the children to tone down their own sharpness of accusations[125] as they learn again and again that your job is to help them communicate the three steps so they can make Shalom. Your gentle tone will help them through these steps and in the end, help them walk away feeling stronger in themselves for not letting the conflict escalate beyond two generations of accusations.

Teacher - Ask Shimon - "*did you do the right thing to call Reuven dumb?*"
Shimon knows it was wrong, he may not be ready to admit it, but by role playing many such scenarios with the class in advance, they will know where you are going with your questions and deep down appreciate you for helping them let go of anger, revenge, resentment, multi-generational accusations and learn to control their thoughts and behavior.

---

124 Igrot Moshe, Yoreh Deah, Cheleck Sheni, Siman #103.
125 See Mishley 15:1 - מַעֲנֶה־רַּךְ יָשִׁיב חֵמָה - 'A soft answer turns around anger' meaning that when a person is provoked to anger and replies with a soft, gentle voice, he can actually tones down the anger of himself and the person who is angry with him (This is how Rabeynu Yona on Mishley 14:30 explains this Passuk). See also Koheles 11:10.

Shimon might answer - "*No! But Reuven tore my picture*" (2nd Generation).
You do *not* want to ask Reuven "*why he tore Shimon's paper?*"
Shimon jolly well knows he did not do the right thing to call Reuven dumb, but right now, in his outrage, he is still hurt because his picture is torn, he thought he would get back at Reuven by calling him dumb and innocently and mistakenly thinks he had to 'get even' with Reuven.

Teacher to Shimon: "*So when we do something wrong, what should we do?*"
If Shimon is ready to apologize he may say: "*I should apologize to Reuven for calling him dumb.*"
You are the teacher, read Shimon's body language and facial expression, if you see Shimon is still angry about his torn picture and really does not look like he wants to apologize, give him room with a question:

"*Shimon, do you want more time before saying what you think you should say to Reuven?*" "*Shall I ask you again in five minutes, or do you need more time, like 8 or 10 minutes till you are ready?*"

By showing Shimon you respect his process of needing time, he will more likely cooperate and either apologize now or ask for 5 - 10 minutes space. He realizes you will revisit the need for him to apologize and you are not letting go on that.

If you have play roled these scenarios in class time, Shimon will know that your next step is to ask Reuven the same soul searching questions, so Shimon will not think Reuven is 'off the hook.' Shimon and Reuven will both know you are helping them resolve this B'Shalom and not taking sides.

Step 2b - Ask Reuven did he do the right thing to...
Teacher asks Reuven
"*Did you do the right thing to tear Shimon's picture?*"
Again, you are focusing on the child's response (tearing the picture), not what was done to him (Reuven called Shimon Dumb).

Step 3 - Ask "What should you do?" (Say Sorry - Apologize).
3.a. Solicit Reuven's apology
Once you have heard Reuven say he was wrong to tear Shimon's picture then ask him *"what should you do if you do something wrong?"*[126]

If Reuven is ready, he will apologize with one word -
"sorry" or
"sorry I tore your picture" or
"I am really sorry I tore your picture, please forgive me!"

Ask Shimon if he forgives Reuven. If he says he does, ask him to say so to Reuven. "*I forgive you Reuven, or I am Mochel you.*"

3.b. Solicit Shimon's apology.
"*Shimon, is there something you want to say to Reuven for calling him a name* (dumb)." Most likely Shimon will follow suit with Reuven and say sorry and ask for forgiveness, at which point you can ask Reuven if he forgives Shimon.
If he forgives Shimon, then have them shake hands and see how they bounce back to play together or go back happily to what they were doing before, letting the entire incident be buried and forgotten (kids are measurably better at bouncing back than we adults!).

There is a step 4 which the teacher can use his/her discretion to *decide if the children are ready for*. This is a straight forward question about reflection on what they did. The teacher simply asks "What could you have done instead?" or "what other ways could you have handled the conflict?"

Step 4. What could you have done instead? What could you do next time?

Teacher to Shimon -
- "*What could you have done instead?*" (instead of calling Reuven dumb).

---

126 Reuven does not need to be told "you are a bad boy" or "that was very wrong of you" or "go the corner" or "no recess for a week!" etc etc. Reuven can come to the right conclusion by himself. He can recognize his mistake and say sorry himself, thus fulfilling the Mitzvah of being mekabel Tochacha and doing Teshuva by saying sorry. Any giving of 'punishment' is missing the entire purpose of the Torah's view of Tochacha or Onesh. Tochacha means to *clarify*. Onesh really means to 'see how I went wrong.' The last two letters of ענש are נש - the two letter root of falling (like נשל - fall, or נשר - an eagle which swoops '*down*.' The first letter ע of ענש means 'eye.' The meaning of ענש is to *see* how I have *fallen*, to see where I went wrong (heard from Rabbi Shimon Schwab z"l).

Possible responses:
- "*I could have said why did you tear my picture, it's my property, not yours!?* or
- "*That was not nice*" or
- "*Why did you tear my picture, I worked a long time on it!?*"
- "*I could ignore Reuven and start another picture.*"

Teacher to Reuven -
- "*What could you have done instead?*" (of tearing his picture).
- "*I could have asked Shimon why he called me dumb*" or
- "*I could have asked Shimon if he he called me dumb because I tore up his picture?*" or
- "*I could have written him a note saying I am really sorry that I tore his picture, let's make Shalom!*"

In summary, this is the formula for Tochacha:
1. Collect information, What Happened? Who claims what!
2a. Ask Shimon if he did the right thing to....
2b. Ask Reuven if he did the right thing to....
3a. Ask Reuven what he should do (apologize)
3b. Ask Shimon what he should do (apologize)
4. Ask What could you do instead in the future?

And *Shalom Al Yisrael*! There will always be slight variations of this formula. Sometimes you may have Reuven making a claim he believes is true but it turns out that Shimon was not the student who hurt Reuven but someone else. Or Reuven had said an insult to a different student and Shimon thought Reuven was speaking to him!

The main point here is to
1. Allow both sides to be heard up until two generations of accusations and then...
2. Ask if they responded correctly by hurting back, or calling a name, or insulting his family, etc. Then have them...
3. Recognize their mistake and apologize.

3.8 Examples of applying Tochacha - Using Puppets[127]

Role-play scenarios of conflict using puppets so that it is depersonalized. Do this at the beginning of the school year every morning in circle time, with the entire class. Then they can role play between themselves with the puppets.

'The Tochacha - Shalom Puppets.'

Another option is to actually label two puppets in the classroom '*The Tochacha - Shalom Puppets.*' When a child is upset with another child, he can take the two puppets and hold one while giving the other puppet to the child who wronged him. He then tells his friend (through the puppet he is holding) this issue he is upset about and his friend responds using his puppet.

The rule in the class is if you are given a puppet, you have to accept it and listen to what the other puppet asks you (e.g "Why did you tear my picture?"). Then they go through the same 3-Step Tochacha Formula as above.

Here are examples of scenarios the children can re-enact with the puppets, using the Tochacha Formula:

- You pushed me in recess!
- You kicked me!
- You took my snack!
- You said my mother is always late for car pool!
- You called me a bad name!
- You said a bad word to me first!
- You said I talk funny!
- You said my Mum is fat!
- You tore my homework!
- You said I smell!
- You broke your promise!
- You lied to me!
- You called me stupid!
- You scribbled all over my picture!
- You said when I am picked on your team you always lose!

---

[127] Please note that in the DVD version, this section of applying Tochacha using Puppets appears in 3.4. The numbering in this document is slightly different because we added more background information and sources from the Torah than in the DVD.

4.0
Metaphors to Understand How My Middos come from Thought. Reality Vs Non-Reality Thinking

Listed below are many metaphors. Some are very brief activities and others are in story format (Mashal) with a lesson (Nimshal) for the children to extrapolate.

We suggest giving one metaphor a week for the duration of the school year.

Each metaphor is reinforcing how all Middos Tovos and Ra'os are sourced in thought in the moment.

The accumulation of this message every week, that our Middos are shaped by our thinking, will begin to take root in the students' minds and you will notice changes in their own behavior and attitudes as the school year progresses.

Each metaphor is designed to dramatize and concretize how we live inside thought every moment and how the Torah wants us to be aware of our thinking so we can make better choices.

4.1 Metaphor # 1:
Your Innate Health, Neshama,[128] is always communicating to you.

Goal:
Experience how thought in the moment can cover up my innate health and resilience but never silence it.
The music is always playing, even when it is muffled or seemingly silenced by thought in the moment.

Note to teacher: Before you do this impressionist lesson, check how many towels/cloths will be needed to silence the soft music coming from the CD or phone. Then you will know how many towels/cloths to distribute between the number of students in your group.

Props for this Experiential Metaphor:
1. CD player or Phone with soft music
2. Towels/cloths/small blankets
3. Safety pins
4. Paper
5. Pen

---

[128] You may prefer to use the term - Innate Health or Reality-Thoughts or Inside-Out-Thoughts.

Step 1.
Play very soft, relaxing music (or select such music to play on your phone).

Step 2.
Ask the students to each draw a picture of a thought bubble with room in the middle of the bubble to write a negative thought.

Ask them to write a thought they do not like inside their bubble, for example:[129]
- *Fear*
- *Anxiety*
- *I have no friends*
- *My life is a such a mess*
- *I'm such a slob*
- *Why can't I ever lose weight?*
- *I am so slow*
- *I am so dumb*
- *I'm a loser*
- *Why are my school friends so nasty to me?*
- *I hate my brother*
- *My sister is such a nerd*
- *My Mum totally does not understand me*

Step 3.
Ask the students to come and take a towel/cloth and a safety pin, and then pin their thought bubble to their towel/cloth.[130]

Step 4.
Have each student come in turn to the front of the class with their thought bubble pinned to their towel/cloth and read out loud what they wrote inside the thought bubble and then place the cloth over the CD player/Phone.

Each time a student covers the music, the music becomes a drop more faint.

Do the same with yet another student, towel/cloth etc, as many times till the music is no longer audible from the many layers of towels/cloths.

---

[129] Tweak the examples you give the children according to their age and their culture.
[130] If there are 20 students and 10 towels, then ask the students to pin two thought bubbles per towel.

Step 5.1
Invite the students to extrapolate the lessons they see in this impressionist metaphor.

If they are not responsive, tell the children:
- "*The music is your Neshama, your innate health*, it is always playing and communicating softly."
- "Your Neshama always knows that you are loved in Hashem's eyes, you are His child."
- "Your Neshama always knows Hashem never makes a mistake, and runs His world perfectly."
- "Your Neshama knows that גם זו לטובה is reality! Your Neshama is afraid of nothing."
- "Your Neshama lives forever and and can never be destroyed."

Then a 'Yetzer Hara thought' of anxiety comes to mind, slightly muffling the sound of the music.

Then another 'Yetzer Hara' thought of worry, then another of fear cover the music till all can you hear are the thoughts covering the sound of your innate health.

But as you realize the music is truly still there, your Yetzer HaTov thoughts are always ready to pop up in your next thought, then you become willing to not let the interfering Yetzer Hara thoughts paint your reality. Yetzer Tov thoughts are music to your ears, insights into yourself, insights to let you see more, calm your mind more…so it can find its own innate health when you are ready to hear it.

Step 5.2
Ask the students to share examples of 'blanket thoughts' drowning the music (for example, thoughts of hate, or jealousy, or resentment, or fear, or revenge.

Step 5.3
Let them articulate how such thoughts hurt and cover up the music always playing beneath.

Step 5.4
Ask the students what 'blanket thoughts' are most common in their minds.

Step 5.5
Ask them if they remember ignoring thoughts, or ignoring thoughts they did not like and what music (insight) did they hear?

4.2 Metaphor #2:
What options do you have when a pop up shows on the screen of your phone?

Goal:
See how thoughts are like pop-ups, and I really have a choice to explore or ignore.

Props:
1. iPhone
2. White board and markers/large blown up photo of an iPhone with empty screen
3. Pack of Post-Its

Step 1.
Draw the outline of an iPhone on the white board.
Or pin on the wall a large blown up photo of an iPhone with nothing on the screen.

Step 2.
Ask the students what options they have when they get a pop up on the screen of their phone? They will tell you - "exit or open!" Or we can call it:
A. **Explore** or
B. **Ignore**

Step 3.
Ask the students to close their eyes for 20 seconds and try to stop thinking!

After 20 seconds, ask them to tell you what they noticed.
Tell them '*your thoughts are exactly like pop ups*,' you really cannot stop them. They just keep popping up! Your thoughts never stop! Your mind was created to always be turned on to thinking mode! Try not thinking! It's not possible!

But what you do next is your free will. 'Explore or Ignore!?'
Do you open the pop up thought and explore it some, or think about it a lot, and then add on every other cross reference?[131]

---

[131] Like a pop up thought about why you don't like someone and then you get another pop up 'cross-reference' of another thought, another memory of that person being unkind, so now you have two thoughts to justify why you do not like him/her. And your thoughts keep finding new cross-reference pop-pups to strengthen your dislike or even hatred of that person. But in reality, these pop-ups are simply thoughts in the moment, and we are encouraged to look at the good side of others as more real than our speculative thoughts.

Or do you press X and 'Delete' the pop up? The answer is - your choice!

Where is the delete button in your mind? The very next thought!

When we say **your *delete button* is *your very next thought***, that means three options:

Option #1
You do not continue thinking about the pop-up in your next thought, instead you **distract yourself with a different thought**, making a phone call, do your homework, get busy with a business task, call a friend, write an email, shop for the family, etc.[132]

Option #2
You simply turn the next moment into a **Tefilah of thanks**.[133] Here are eight simple examples of turning non-reality thoughts into Todah to Hashem:
1. "Thank you Hashem for giving me my Yetzer Hara for me to ignore and gain more favor in Your eyes."
2. "Thank You Hashem for the Yetzer Hara so I can turn to *You* instead of listening to my Yetzer, so that the Yetzer Hara makes me come closer to You."
3. "Thank You Hashem for my Yetzer Hara so I can get the Mitzvah of לא תתורו אחרי לבבכם for not listening to my Yetzer when it pop-ups."
4. "Thank You Hashem for my Yetzer Hara because now I get the awesome Mitzvah of Emuna, knowing You are behind my Yetzer to invite me to ignore it!"
5. "Thank You Hashem for the Yetzer Hara because now I can live the Madreiga of being Davuk to You - ובו תדבק and another Mitzvah of בכל דרכיך דעהו, to be aware of You in every direction I go in. Even when my Yetzer Hara attacks me with non-reality thinking, I can win against it by thanking You in my next thought for making me grow through the Yetzer Hara!"
6. "Thank You Hashem for my Yetzer Hara because now I get the awesome Mitzvah of showing my love for You with my Yetzer Hara!"[134]

---

132 See Likutei Moharan II 50, #51 110. See also Chayey Moharan #44, 506.
133 The concept of thanking Hashem for a challenge in life is actually based on Shulchan Aruch, Orach Chaim, Siman #222:3. See also Tur #222 and Brachos 9:5. The main message is that one has an obligation to thank Hashem for seemingly bad situations with the same Simcha as when being grateful to Hashem for the obvious good we are blessed with.

7. "Thank You Hashem for my Yetzer Hara because now I get the Mitzvah of not believing any other power exists except You! Because my Yetzer Hara makes me turn to You to save me instead of believing anything else can help me without Your help!"
8. "Thank You Hashem for my Yetzer Hara thought because now I get the Mitzvah of the Shema Yisrael when I say You are Echud, it means You Are the Only One Force in all creation, so by thanking You for my Yetzer I am saying You sent me my Yetzer to test my love for you and to say ONLY YOU are the ONE Source of everything!

Option #3
In your next thought, **ask Hashem a One Line Tefila:**
"Please help me ignore my non-reality thinking."
"Please Hashem, help me ignore my Yetzer Hara, my non-reality thoughts."
"Please help me distract myself to something worthwhile instead of letting my thoughts hurt me!"
"Please Help me just turn to You with a thank You!"

Step 4.
Ask the students to each write just one pop-up thought on a Post It and bring it to the illustration on the white board or hanging photo of the iphone and post it on the screen of the iphone.

Step 5.
Read each Post-It aloud and ask for a show of hands whether we should explore or ignore?
Ask *"who wants to tell us why they voted to ignore"*?
Ask *"who wants to tell us why they voted to explore"*?

You want to guide the students to notice how our thoughts are carried away with the 'explore' option and how our minds are liberated when we select 'ignore' or 'delete.'

You want to guide the students to articulate their own insight of how pop-ups are really thought in the moment and we truly have the power to control our next thought in response to the thoughts popping up in our mind in the moment.

---

134 The Mitzvah to love Hashem is found in Dev. 6:5 - וְאָהַבְתָּ אֵת ה' אֱלֹקֶיךָ בְּכָל־לְבָבְךָ which Chazal tell us in Brachos 9:5 means to love Hashem with both your Yetzer Hara thoughts and Yetzer Tov thoughts - בִּשְׁנֵי יְצָרֶיךָ, בְּיֵצֶר טוֹב וּבְיֵצֶר רָע.

If you feel the students are ready, you can share the following:
When I find something really challenging (a Nissayon) it's probably because I cannot stop thinking about it.[135] I keep exploring it from many angles.

Each time I think about the pop-up thought, the more I am exploring the pop-up, the more the screen of my mind is filled with more thoughts of anxiety, worry, fear, speculations, doubts and concern, anger or even hatred and resentment!

Once I know my thought is ONLY A POP-UP! I am free to make a better choice because my thoughts are literally in my hand to press delete or open, ignore or explore! Where is the 'delete' button of my mind? The next thought!

If I know this pop-up thought will lead me down the road of more upset, I am more likely to select X and delete the thought sooner! I feel in control. Even though I will probably get another pop up, I simply feel in control *just now* because I know I am the one who can delete or explore!

Nobody can make me think what I don't want to think!

- Ask the students to share what pop-ups they don't like the most.
- Ask for volunteers to keep a personal log of their pop ups and responses to share next week. Tell them they will be invited, if they want, to share what difference they noticed in their thinking because they now know their thoughts are only pop-ups in the moment and in one touch (the next thought) you can delete it, ignore it!

Ask the students for any insights they have had since last week?

---

135 For example, a friend who said an *unkind word*, or *my parent does not understand me*, or *my sister/brother is always annoying me*, or *my teacher does not show appreciation for my hard work*, etc.

4.3 Metaphor #3:
Your mind is like a beautifully kept garden. Sometimes weeds pop up (negative thoughts[136]), what options do you have? Uproot the weeds? Or water them!![137]

Goal:
See the absurdity of letting my mind repeat unhelpful thoughts. This helps leverage oneself to let go sooner of one's non-reality thinking.

Props:
1. White board with color markers
2. Packet of Post-Its
3. Pens

Step 1
Draw a simple illustration of a flower garden on the white board. Draw each flower with a stalk and the outline of empty petals which the children will soon stick their post its on.

Step 2
Tell the following story:
Once upon a time, Mr. A was walking through his beautiful garden, admiring all the wonderful variety of colors. A thought occurred to him. *His mind is like his garden!*
He thought of each family member and personal friend as another colorful flower. He thought of all the people in his life, each one with his/her own color, shape, scent, arrangement of petals, etc,. Mr. A looked at his flowers as though each one represented one of the many blessings he can think of. His health, family, opportunities, love, giving, kindness, his clothes and friends, home, career...etc - One day, he was walking in his garden and he noticed some weeds growing. What should our friend Mr. A do?
1. Ignore the weeds?
2. Uproot them so they do not take over and destroy his beautiful garden? Or
3. Fetch a watering can and begin to water the weeds?!! Imagine! Mr. A decides to water them!

Walking through his garden the next day, he notices the weeds have grown since yesterday, so he waters them some more!!!

---

[136] The Yetzer Hara is usually the negative thoughts, like anger, hatred, jealousy, resentment, etc. See Likutey Moharan, I, Lesson #49 where he writes that
מחשבות רעות הם היצר הרע והמחשבות טובות הם היצר הטוב.
[137] This idea is based on the same metaphor of Rabbi Avigdor Miller.

While Mr. A so busy with the weeds, watering them daily, growing them, his garden is becoming more and more neglected and as he looks at his garden, he keeps focusing on the weeds instead of uprooting them, he innocently waters them by thinking about them!

Step 3
1. Ask the students to share with you/the class examples of blessings in their life right now, what is good about their life right now? Ask them to share as many examples as possible of reasons they are grateful or happy.[138] The reasons can be as simple as my lungs work, I am alive, I was born healthy, my dad has a job, or I can talk, I have no speech impediment. At first this may feel awkward but ask them to identify any good/blessing, virtue or even a happy memory they have of family, friends, school, favorite hobbies, what they are talented at, etc.
2. Ask them to write down each example on a Post-It. Give them 2 minutes to write as many examples of their blessings on post its, one example per Post-It.
3. Take turns for them to come up to the white board and place their post its inside the outline of the empty petals.
4. Tell them "each of these items are just some of the many beautiful flowers in the garden of their mind." Each of these items are thoughts, either in the now, or they are memories that are brought to your mind now.
5. Now ask them to identify a few of the things that are not going right in their lives right now!
6. Ask them to write them on Post-Its. Give them 1 minute to write (it's often easier to think of what is wrong in life than what we are grateful for, so they will not need more than a minute for this!). Then tell them "these are weeds in your garden."
7. Ask them to bring their 'weeds' to the white board and place them around the beautiful flowers.
8. Ask: What should they do to keep their garden beautiful?
9. Ask: What will you tell me if I take a watering can and water the weeds in my garden!" And then I do the same tomorrow, and the next day! Why do you think that makes no sense! Ask them if watering the weeds is logical or ILL - Logical!?
10. Ask the class to share their thoughts about this metaphor.

Ask the students for any insights they have had since last week?

---

[138] See Rabbi Shalom Arush's Sefer Garden of Miracles. Say "Thank You" & See Miracles. 190 true stories about the power of gratitude.

4.4. Metaphor #4:
The gigantic white sheet and the black dot in the middle![139]

Goal:
1. Recognize the fake power of the media to influence our thoughts.
2. Recognize the good in life is always far greater in quantity and quality than whatever appears not good.

Props:
1. Daily newspaper/s or iphone with internet access.
2. Large white sheet of graph paper or just use the white board in the classroom.
3. Black Marker
4. Pack of Post-Its

Step 1
On a clean white board draw a black spot in the middle.
In the absence of a white board, draw a black spot in the middle of a large sheet of white graph paper.[140]

Step 2
Ask the class what do they see?
Most of them will respond with a similar answer, they see a white board with a black spot in the middle or a black spot in the middle of the white board. Say nothing, hold your response to later.

Step 3
Pass a newspaper from today's or yesterday's news and each student takes a turn to read one headline from the front page, and ask if the news is:
1. Good or
2. Bad news or
3. Something else?

After all the headlines have been read on the front page, continue passing the newspaper for the other students to read one headline each from page two and finally page three (assuming three pages of headlines will be enough for all the students to have a turn to read). If you are concerned some children will not want to read out loud to the class, then just invite them generically - "who wants a turn to read the next headline?"
Alternatively, the teacher could access one of the daily newspaper's web site on their iphone/smart phone and each student reads one

---

[139] This idea is based on the same metaphor given by Chief Rabbi Jonathan Sacks.
[140] Preferably a very large sheet, 3 X 4 feet, or use a sheet of white graph paper from a flip chart.

headline at a time and answers the question whether the news is good or bad or something else?

The goals of this part of the presentation is simply for the students to pay attention to the disproportionate representation of bad news versus the good news.

Step 3
Ask the students to write down on a Post-It one example of bad news reported daily.
For example:
Corruption, scandals, murder, death, traumatic events, reports of terrorism, injuries, fatal accidents, car crashes, political back stabbing and bad mouthing, law suits, theft, black mail, suicides, divorce, physical violence, drunken driving, illness, disease, tragedy, domestic violence, scams, etc, etc.

Ask if any students think that people reading/listening to the news every single day might find themselves experiencing fear, outrage, anxiety, desperation, feeling insignificant, at a loss of how the world could ever get better?

Step 4
Ask the students to bring their Post-It to the white board, read it out loud as they stick it beneath the black spot. Let each student do the same, placing their Post-It on top of the previous Post-It so you now see the white board with a black spot in the middle with a stack of Post-Its beneath.

Step 5
Ask: "*Why does the brain look at this large white sheet and immediately notice the black spot in the middle?*"
You can guide them with a similar question: "*what is it about the black spot that immediately catches the eye?*"
You want to guide the students to notice how much more white there is than the black dot.
Typical responses will be something like this:
"*The black spot catches my eye because it stands out,*" or
"*compared to the all-white background, the black spot is in such contrast so it stands out.*"

Step 6

Take the pile of Post-Its and place them *on top of the black spot* and announce:
"***This black spot is bad news!***" Pause a few seconds and then ask
"*Do you know why this is bad news?*"

"Because it's NEWS!!"

Let the answer sink in.

Why does good news not grab our attention?
Because good news is not news!! Good is happening all the time so it is not news.

For every fatal accident on the road, in flight, trains and boats, what proportion of passengers arrive safely at their destination? 99.9% !!

For every theft and robbery, what proportion of the population are not stealing? In the high 90th percentile.

For every fatal illness, how many people die of natural causes and old age?

For every murder, how many children are being born that moment? For every person drowning, what proportion of swimmers come out of the water safely? 99.9%

So if there is so much GOOD NEWS all the time, why does the black spot steal my thoughts? *Because it is NEWS*!

The CLINCHER:
- The black spot is thought!
- When you pay attention to the black spot, it is thought in the moment!
- How long do you think about the black spot?
- As long as you think about it!
- How far are you from moving away from the black thought and noticing the white? Noticing the good news, the happy thoughts of what is good in life?
- You are only one thought away.

When you hit a black spot in your life, what choices do you have? Explore or Ignore! Open or Delete!

Ask the class for their comments.

Step 7
Ask the class for a volunteer/s to keep a log over the next week before the next session to write down any insights he/she had. That means any time they noticed their thoughts switch from black spot - bad news focus to something else.

Announce that next week's session will begin with those students sharing what they wrote.

Five Metaphors to Reveal Children's Inner Resilience

The main goal of the next five metaphors[141] is to have the children experience their own indestructible, innate resilience which is always there inside of them and can never go away or be harmed. We can only forget it is always there, but that will not change the fact that our resilience is immediately ready the moment we know it is there, as when remembering the music of our Neshama is always singing "Life is Really Good!"

This knowledge, that their thought is the true source of their emotions is what will help build their inside-out immunity to many of life's challenges, ranging from sibling rivalry, bullying, domestic abuse, and indeed life's Nisayonos and surprises.

---

[141] These five metaphors are also covered in Building Block #10 Recess under the section on 'Bully-Proof Your Child.'

4.5 Metaphor #5: Is the Spider Real or Fake?

The goal is for the children to articulate how reality is dictated by what I *think* reality is. Not what is actually outside of us.

Scenario A:
"ARRHH, A Spider is on me!!! Oh Phew it was just fake!"

Ask the students "*what made me fear the spider?*"
My thoughts! I *thought* it was a real spider.

Scenario B:
"HUH, very funny! That's my brother playing another practical joke on me!"
You flick the spider off your shoulder and then freak out when you see it scuttle away - *"ARRHHH it was REAL!"*

Ask the students "*what made me not fear the spider?*"
My thoughts! I *thought* it was a fake spider.

So is my fear created by the spider being real or not real?
Or by what my *thoughts* tell me it is?

Have the children discuss this as an opening to the discovery of the true origin of our feelings and experiences.

Ask the students for any insights they have had since last week.

4.6 Metaphor #6: How Much is This Dollar Bill Worth?

The goal
For the children to articulate how nothing outside of them can ever change their true worth.
My true worth is never damaged or can ever be harmed.

After asking the students to crunch and stamp on, shout and insult the bill (see 1-10 below), ask each time if the dollar bill lost its value for the abuse it received or is it still 100% a dollar bill (or 5 or 10 or 20 or 100 dollar bill).

Ask the students:
1. Who is the Bully in the Mashal? And
2. Who is the Target?

The *bully* is the *hand and mouth* that abused the dollar bill while the *bill* is the *Target.*

Ask why they say the dollar bill did not lose its true value?
Have them articulate the dollar value is the inside of the person, their 'thought in the moment,' the Tzelem Elokim which cannot be destroyed.

You want the children to articulate these lessons with your guidance.

Consider giving each child in the class their own newly printed One Dollar bill for this Mashal.

Ask them to:
1. Crunch it up
2. Tell it you hate it
3. Tell it it's ugly
4. Tell it it's dumb and stupid
5. Tell it is worthless
6. Throw it on the floor
7. Stump on it.
8. Pretend to spit on it.
9. Nobody likes you.
10. You have no friends.

Ask each time, how much is it worth now?

Tell parents, they should do this with their own children. If appropriate, consider offering your child a $20, $50 or even $100 dollar bill (depending on how much you think you need this lesson to penetrate your child because you will tell them they get to keep the bill if they can find the right answers deep inside themselves).

For added affect, show the class a swab of clean $10 bills. Give them out to each child in the class. Ask:
- How much is it worth?
- Crumple it! How much is it worth now?
- Throw it on floor, how much is it worth now?
- Tread on it and ask again - How much is it worth now?
- Stamp on it! - How much is it worth now?
- Spit on it! - How much is it worth now?
- Curse it and call it names! Ask again - How much is it worth now?
- Is it still worth $10, then tell me what this lesson teaches you, if he/she answers correctly, then say "it's yours to keep" and let your student/child keep it.

Ask the children what they learned?
Guide them to share the lessons they derived from this activity. Let them surprise you with their insights.

Examples:
- What to tell myself when I am being insulted or bullied.
- How to see through the words of others as just thoughts in the moment.
- How to notice that what they say is not true.
- How to respond to intimidation.
- How I feel immune to their words or opinions because they cannot break my thinking unless I give them permission.

If you are a target of a bully, this is how to help yourself not give the bully more bullets. Here are some examples of responses when coming from Inside-Out:

- "Cool! That's only what you think of me but it is not my thinking of me!"
- "Cool for you, I have a different opinion and I believe in my reality and you believe in yours."
- "Cool! that's your opinion but not mine, your opinion cannot hurt my mind unless I give you power to do so."
- "I'm amused by the irony that they think they have power over me."
- "I smiled inside myself that they are mistaken and their words are only thoughts in my mind which I can ignore if I choose!"

The following topic of discussion is more for upper elementary students:

Depending on the maturity of the students, you can open a discussion about the difference between שתיקה and תדום.
Both translate as 'silence.' So what are the two types of silence?

The silence of שתיקה is not 'showing' the insult (bullet) hit you, even though it did, but you remain silent.[142]
The silence of תדום is you do not even *feel* the pain of the insult because you don't *think* 'pain,' that is the level of the insult not even penetrating you!

You don't let the insult stay with you, (by thinking about it) instead, you let it bounce off.

The most common response to this distinction is that "I am only human!
How can I be so strong to not even *think* about the insult?

Let's briefly examine how the Torah gives a vote of confidence in my ability to control my response to insults, curses, unkind words, etc. The Torah commands me not to hold a grudge against others, which means 'don't recall the wrongs others have done to me.' This is a Lo Taaseh and all Rishonim agree it's one of the Taryag Mitzvos -
Lev. 19:18 - וְלֹא־תִטֹּר אֶת־בְּנֵי עַמֶּךָ
Rashi spells it out even more clearly when describing one who recalls the unkindliness of his friend, he still remembers the wrong done to him instead of letting go of the memory![143] - שהדבר שמור בלבו, ולא הסיחו מדעתו
'He still holds onto the memory and does not let go of thinking about it.'
When we look closely at the entire verse where this command is found, we could be quite baffled!
לֹא־תִקֹּם וְלֹא־תִטֹּר אֶת־בְּנֵי עַמֶּךָ וְאָהַבְתָּ לְרֵעֲךָ כָּמוֹךָ אֲנִי ה'

---

142 Avot 4:3 - gives two definitions of a Gibor, a powerful person. First it is one who conquers his Yetzer, his anger, because the verse states that 'one who is patient is greater than a powerful person. His patience is indicated by the fact that he has been provoked to anger but is holding in the breath in his nostrils, corresponding to the first level of silence we just mentioned - אֵיזֶהוּ גִבּוֹר, הַכּוֹבֵשׁ אֶת יִצְרוֹ, שֶׁנֶּאֱמַר (משלי טז), טוֹב אֶרֶךְ אַפַּיִם מִגִּבּוֹר.
But the verse now offers a second level of silence, of the one who is provoked to anger but does not so much as change a heartbeat, literally "he controls his breath" וּמֹשֵׁל בְּרוּחוֹ מִלֹּכֵד עִיר . So we see how both levels of silence are indicated by the passuk in Mishley 16:32.
143 Yuma 23a top of the Daf.

There are three Mitzvos from Taryag in this one verse:
1. Don't take revenge - לֹא־תִקֹּם
2. Don't recall other people's unkindliness to you - וְלֹא־תִטֹּר
3. Love other Jews like you love yourself - וְאָהַבְתָּ לְרֵעֲךָ כָּמוֹךָ

The glaring question is, how can the Torah command me in one verse to shift from the deep rage of wanting *revenge* and holding a *grudge* to *loving* everyone?!

Would the Torah not have been more understanding toward us had it put revenge and holding a grudge near the beginning of Bereishis and love your neighbor near the end of Devarim and give me some space to recover!!?

The simple, yet profound answer, is that revenge is a *thought*.

You only live one thought at a time.
Holding a grudge, remembering someone elses unkindliness to me is a *thought*.

Loving another Jew is a *thought*.

Hashem is telling us that we are able to go from one thought to the next! Even though they are extremely different thoughts. The proof Hashem knows we can, is *He designed us* and so *He* can tell us to recognize the origin of my revenge and baring a grudge are both *thought* in the moment.

I can always change my next thought, even to one of Ahava, love. And if I doubt for a moment that I have such power, Hashem signs His Name at the end of the Passuk to indicate, "I know you can do this, because אֲנִי ה' - I Am Hashem YKVK!" So don't question whether you are able to control your next thought! Yes - You can! because **I HASHEM** say you can!

Bullying is all about who looks more cool. What does the coolest kid (bully) win? He wins power.

- But what is real power? Is real power your physical muscles or your internal muscles? What are internal muscles? Your inner resilience to stand up to adversity and inner resilience to get up after you are knocked down.

- Real Power is an inside job, and kids deep down really know this truth. Deep down they know they are much stronger than the bully, deep down we all know we are NOT VICTIMS, ever!
- Deep down, we actually know that even the bully is not a bully, he is also only living in thought of the moment and can turn himself around in the next thought.

Encourage your students to turn the bullying comments into a Tefila to Hashem. Here are some options:
You simply turn the next moment into a **Tefilah of thanks**.[144] Here are eight simple examples of turning thoughts that make us feel intimidated by others into Todah to Hashem:

1. "Thank you Hashem for the invitation to be silent to those who hurt me with words because now I can prove to You and myself how strong I am inside."
2. "Thank You Hashem for the bully because now I can turn to *You* instead of listening to my thoughts of fear, so the bully and my fear thoughts (Yetzer Hara) make me come closer to You."
3. "Thank You Hashem for the bully so I can get the Mitzvah of אמונה because I know everything comes from You because You love me. Now I will be stronger in my Emuna because of the bully!"
4. Thank You Hashem for the bully because now I can live the Mitzvah of being Davuk to You - ובו תדבק and another Mitzvah of בכל דרכיך דעהו, to be aware of You in every direction I go in.
5. "Thank You Hashem for bully because now I get the awesome Mitzvah of showing my love for You when I have thoughts of fear"[145]
6. "Thank You Hashem for the bully because now I get the Mitzvah of not believing any other power exists except You![146] Because my Yetzer Hara makes me turn to You to save me instead of believing anything else can help me without Your help!"
7. In your next thought, you can **ask Hashem** "Please help me ignore both the bully and the fear I have of him."
8. "Thank You Hashem for my Yetzer Hara thought because now I get the Mitzvah of the Shema Yisrael when I say You are Echud, it means You Are the Only One Force in all creation, so by thanking

---

[144] The concept of thanking Hashem for a challenge in life is actually based on Shulchan Aruch, Orach Chaim, Siman #222:3. See also Tur #222 and Brachos 9:5. The main message is that one has an obligation to thank Hashem for seemingly bad situations with the same Simcha as when being grateful to Hashem for the obvious good we are blessed with.

[145] The Mitzvah to love Hashem is found in Dev. 6:5 - וְאָהַבְתָּ אֵת ה' אֱלֹקֶיךָ בְּכָל־לְבָבְךָ which Chazal tell us in Brachos 9:5 means to love Hashem with both your Yetzer Hara thoughts and Yetzer Tov thoughts - בִּשְׁנֵי יְצָרֶיךָ, בְּיֵצֶר טוֹב וּבְיֵצֶר רָע.

[146] This is the second Mitzvah in the Aseret HaDibros - Ex.20:3 - לֹא־יִהְיֶה לְךָ אֱלֹהִים אֲחֵרִים עַל־פָּנָי. Not to believe any other powers exist except Hashem.

You for my Yetzer I am saying You sent me my Yetzer to test my love for you and to say ONLY YOU are the ONE Source of everything!

Ask the students for any insights they have had since last week?

4.7 Metaphor #7: Ten-Pin Bowling

The Goal
1. To experience the power struggle between external power (a bully trying to knock you down with his bowl) and the inner resilience of a Bowling Pin that is grounded in Emet, reality of who you are, Tzelem Elokim.

You cannot be knocked down because thoughts cannot knock you down unless you give them that power to *think* you are knocked down!

2. Experience how the bully will go elsewhere when faced with a target that won't fall because the bully has no power against this pin/target.

For added affect:
Have the kids play 10 pin with a set of plastic pins and a bowel.
Then nail a pin into a board so that it is nailed tight onto its floor board.
Throw the ball at the pin which is nailed down and ask the children, why does the pin not fall when hit?

Ask them to explain what is happening. Ask the children to describe what the metaphor means. If needed, ask them to identify who is the bully and who is the target in this metaphor.

1. The Pin is the Target
2. The Bowler is the Bully
3. The Bowel is the insult

Have the children share their insights.

- If the bully knocks down even one pin, he is on his way to winning, and he will throw another bowel.
- If the bully does not knock down any pins, he does not look cool because the pins are more powerful, so the TARGET WINS. Bully gives up and goes elsewhere.
- How does the bully know he has no power over you?
- How do you feel when you let your inner resilience stand you strong?
- What are examples of how your inner power comes out?

Examples of how your inner resilience will surface when the non-reality thinking disappears:
- Laughing off criticism = all ten Pins are still standing.
- Smiles in face of adversity.
- Makes a new friend.
- Stands up for himself without whining, pleading, or insulting back.
- Tells the bully 'whatever he says does not matter, it does not change your reality!' (Because you know you are Tzelem Elokim and Hashem is with you everywhere, all the time and Hashem is The One behind the bully, so all you need do is turn to Hashem in Tefila, which is either thank you, praise or a request).[147]
- SHOW no emotion, raise your eyebrows as if to say "okay, but what you say does not change me!"

Ask the students for any insights they have had since last week?

---

[147] See end of 4.6 above for examples of one line Thank Yous to Hashem and a Tefila for asking Hashem to help you reveal your inner resilience without falling to the bullying of the bully.

4.8 Metaphor #8: A Rolls Royce Vs a 67 Chevy[148]

The Goal
To identify Who Am I? Who is the real me?

Q: Is the real me my body, my car, my clothes, my house, my family, my job, my money, my friends, my community?
Q: Or is the real me a THINKING SOUL, Powered by Tzelem Elokim?

We will use the metaphor of a Rolls Royce in contrast to a bashed up Chevy to bring out the contrast between fake identity and true identity.

Who Am I? A Rolls Royce or beat up Chevy?
No matter what you call me, you can't change who I truly am, I'm a Rolls Royce.

If I think I am a bashed up 67' Chevy and you insult me, scratch me, kick, well! I'm already an old beat up car, so what difference will another scratch, dent or kick do? I'm all bashed up anyway!?

But if I believe I am a Rolls Royce, as soon as you even come near me with the look of wanting to scratch or dent me, I will yell out "What on earth do you think you are doing? I'm a Rolls Royce?"
And even if they succeed in kicking or denting or scratching the Rolls, does that mean I am no longer a Rolls Royce?

What if I really am so beat up, covered in scratches and dents that I believe what everyone has told me all these years, that I am a beat up 67' Chevy?

What if I am then taken to the scrap yard for appraisal for useless scrap metal, because that is all I believe I am worth, and the boss of the scrap yard opens the bonnet and cries out, "whow! This is no 67 Chevy, look at the engine, this is a Rolls Royce!?

Now What? What are the implications of this? I was a Rolls Royce all along and did not know it? The body might be badly scarred, but the inside, the engine, the Tzelem Elokim powering your mind is always unscratched.

Ask the students to share their insights on this metaphor.

Ask the students for any insights they have had since last week?

---

[148] You may consider updating the title to a Rolls Royce Vs a 92' Camry.

4.9 Metaphor #9:
Think It Over, But Don't Over-Think It!
The Problem is not the Real Problem!
The Real Problem is the Over-Weight Thinking!

The Goal
To notice how much my *over-thinking* about my problems weighs more than the actual problem/nissayon.

Props
Stack of books or stack of wooden blocks.

Act out the following but let your students know you will be asking them to act this out in pairs.

Step 1.
Take a single book in your hand (can be wooden blocks for more effect or anything really). Tell your students, "*this is my peckle in life, my nissayon. This is my test. Hashem has perfectly designed my Nissayon to be not a drop more than I can carry.*"

Now start telling the students your thoughts out loud, and with every groan, moan and complaint, add another book or wooden block (or whatever you use) to the pile you are carrying.

Gradually show your pain and distress in your face as you add each weight with each thought and slowly bend your knees more and more till you are evidently being crushed by the weight of all you are carrying! So, for example, say out loud:

- 'This is not easy! Why do others have it easier than I?' (add another book/wooden block to your pile)
- 'My brother is such a pain, I wish he was not in our family' (add another book/wooden block to your pile)
- 'Your Mum is so nice, mine is always on top of me for everything I do.' (add another book/wooden block to your pile)
- 'I hate school, I never get good marks, no matter how hard I try.' (add another book/wooden block to your pile)
- 'I don't like my nose, it's too long! too short, too big, too small!" (add another book/wooden block to your pile)
- 'Why can't I ever lose weight?' (add another book/wooden block to your pile)
- 'Oh I have so much anxiety.' (add another book/wooden block to your pile)
- 'Will I ever be rid of this pain?' (add another book/wooden block to your pile)

- 'I wish our family was as wealthy as Ploni.' (add another book/wooden block to your pile)
- 'I wish I had her looks.' (add another book/wooden block to your pile)
- 'Hashem, why do things always happen to me? It's not fair!' (add another book/wooden block to your pile)
- 'I feel so down, I'm such a failure, I have no friends.' (add another book/wooden block to your pile)
- 'I'm terrible at sports, I'm always chosen last on the teams.' (add another book/wooden block to your pile)
- 'Etc, etc, etc.' (with each etc, add another book/wooden block to your pile)

Ask the students to choose a partner and role play the same acting out over-weight thoughts.

Ask the students for their insights after they do this exercise with a partner.

Ask them to tell the class how they were feeling as they added on more groans and weights.

Guide them to recognize how their thoughts about their challenges were weighing them down, and not the actual challenge itself.

Talk about the true mechanics of a Nissayon, how a Nissayon is much harder when we *over-think* about it. We add on so much more weight to our actual baggage till it is so overwhelming that we fill our minds with over-weight thoughts and then complain we are overwhelmed!

Platform from this into a discussion of how Avraham Avinu was able to stand up to all his ten tests. Show them what Rashi reveals (Avot. 5:3) that Avraham did NOT THINK,[149] that is precisely the way to get through tests! By just living and not thinking about the hardship.

Ask the students for any insights they have had since last week

---

149 This is the lashon of Rashi there: שלא הרהר אחרי מדותיו של הקב"ה מרוב אהבתו ממנו. Rashi reveals that the key to Avraham Avinu being עומד בנסיון was because he did not think or second guess Hashem's intent after hearing His Nevua to bring his son as a Korban Olah. See also Rashi Ex. 6:9 Where Hashem compares the Avot who did not even think of questioning Hashem. All three Avot were promised Eretz Yisrael as an inheritance, but Avraham never thought of questioning Hashem when he had to pay a fortune to buy a buriel plot for Sarah, or Yitzchak who had to dig new wells each time they were contested or Yaakov who had to pay for a plot of land to pitch his tent. Each could have wondered why Hashem promised them the entire land of Canaan and yet had to pay for the smallest amount of land! - וּכְשֶׁבִּקֵּשׁ אַבְרָהָם לִקְבּוֹר אֶת שָׂרָה לֹא מָצָא קֶבֶר עַד שֶׁקָּנָה בְּדָמִים מְרֻבִּים, וְכֵן בְּיִצְחָק עִרְעֲרוּ עָלָיו עַל הַבְּאֵרוֹת אֲשֶׁר חָפַר, וְכֵן בְּיַעֲקֹב "וַיִּקֶן אֶת חֶלְקַת הַשָּׂדֶה" (בראשית לג:יט) לִנְטוֹת אָהֳלוֹ, **וְלֹא הִרְהֲרוּ אַחַר מִדּוֹתַי**, וְאַתָּה אָמַרְתָּ "לָמָה הֲרֵעֹתָה" (שמות רבה;סנהדרין קיא). See also Rashi Gen. 17:1 - הִתְהַלֵּךְ לְפָנַי וֶהְיֵה תָמִים. **הָיָה שָׁלֵם בְּכָל נִסְיוֹנוֹתָי.**

4.10 Metaphor #10:
My Palace is My Mind![150] Select your own paintings and furnishings!

Goal:
Recognize the power of thought to shape my mind.

Props:
- White board of Flip Chart
- Post its

Step 1.
Go around the class and ask each student in turn to tell you a word that is a happy word. Write down each word on the white board/black board/flip chart.

Step 2.
Go around the class and ask each student in turn to tell you an unhappy word.
Write each one on the board, in a separate column.

Step 3.
Ask each student to write on a Post-it, their favorite happy word from the list on the board and their most unfavorable and unhappy word on a different Post-it.

Step 4.
Draw a picture on the board of a room with furniture and a bare wall.
Ask the students to come up to the board, one at at time and stick their Post-it on the wall part of the room.

Step 5. Guided Questions
Tell them "this wall is one of many in the palace of their minds!" Ask - "What could they do if unhappy thoughts 'pop up' on the walls of their minds?"

Ask "in what way is your mind your palace?"
Help guide them to the answer:

Ask where do you truly live? In your house? Or is your house where your body lives?

Where does the *real you* reside?

---

[150] This idea is based on the same metaphor of Rabbi Avigdor Miller z"l explaining Proverbs 15:15.

The real you is your mind, powered by your Neshama, powered by Divine Intelligence.

Your mind is where you spend your entire life, you live inside THOUGHT.

Tell the students "You actually have a perfect memory!"
Your Neshama hears and sees everything and never forgets anything![151]
Your mind prints every image you see on the walls of your mind. Every word you hear is written as a caption beneath every image.

And just like a real palace, you decide how to decorate your mind!

If you don't like certain pictures, you can take them down!
Or at the very least, re-write the caption beneath the picture and you change the meaning of the picture. That different meaning will change the thinking and feelings associated with that picture!

Dr. Victor Frankel in his groundbreaking work on Logo-Therapy[152] wrote in his famous book 'Man's Search for Meaning' that the images of the past which pop into your mind will only give you pain if the meaning you give that memory is associated to pain. But the good news is, you can always give a different meaning to your memories! Thus changing what you think and feel about them. Even traumatic memories can be changed by giving a different meaning to what you have been through!

Mishlei 15:15
All the days of the poor man are bad! But a good mind is at a constant banquet!

כָּל־יְמֵי עָנִי רָעִים וְטוֹב־לֵב מִשְׁתֶּה תָמִיד

The second half of the verse reveals the type of poverty described in the first half. Shlomo Hamelech is not referring to material poverty in the word עני (poor man) because that would be too obvious, of course the poor man has a hard life. If it referred to material poverty, the second half of the verse should read '*but all the days of the **rich** man are good!*' The words 'וְטוֹב־לֵב מִשְׁתֶּה תָמִיד' reveal that we are referring to poverty of the mind!

Bava Basra 145b
טוֹב־לֵב מִשְׁתֶּה תָמִיד - ר' ינאי אומר - **זה שדעתו יפה**

---

151 Rashi Ex.22:25, see also Targum on Koheles 12:13.
152 The word 'Logo' is the Greek and later Latin word for 'Meaning'. Therapy means healing. Log-Therapy means healing oneself through selecting the meaning you want to give your experiences.

וְרַבִּי יְהוֹשֻׁעַ אָמַר - כָּל־יְמֵי עָנִי רָעִים - **זה שדעתו קצרה**
טוֹב־לֵב מִשְׁתֶּה תָמִיד - **זה שדעתו רחבה**

דעתו קצרה - narrow mind - because it does not see beyond the moment, as in the expression 'tunnel vision,' or 'short-sighted,' 'limited scope,' not seeing the context and making a bad decision one's limited vision.

דעתו רחבה - Broad mind - Sees a bigger picture, can see all the white and not just the black dot! Knows how life is experienced in thought in the moment 100% of the time. A broad mind means one sees a larger context to the details of life and therefore can make better decisions.

Ask the students for examples of 'poor thinking.' If they need prompting, remind them of how we divide our thoughts in Reality-Thoughts and Non-Reality-Thoughts.

Ask them to explain why 'poor-thinking' is not reality. Examples:

Reality-Thoughts
- Emuna
- Trust in Hashem (Bitachon)
- Love for Hashem
- Love for every Jew
- Yiras Hashem
- Love for Torah
- Love for Mitzvos
- Love for Talimidei Chachamim and Tzadikim
- Hashem is Echad, One
- Judge others favorably
- Simcha
- Gratitude
- Praise for Hashem
- Emulating Hashem

Non-Reality Thoughts
- Anger
- Anxiety
- Fear
- Hatred
- Resentment
- Arrogance
- Revenge
- Negative judgements
- Jealousy
- Ta'ava, desire for unhealthy food

- Ta'ava, desire for money
- Ta'ava for drink

Ask the students for any insights they have had since last week?

4.11 Metaphor #11:
The WWWW.Con (The World Wide Web of Waste.CON)

Goal:
Recognize the power of your mind to shut out the media.

Story
Once upon a time, your neighbor connected his sewer pipe to a hose and knocks on your front door. You let your neighbor in and brings his hose and begins to hose your house with the liquid and solid waste all over your walls, floor and furniture!

When there was no more waste left in the hose, your neighbor apologized that he ran out of waste but will refill and be back soon!!

He came back a few minutes later and knocks on your door, you let him in and he began hosing waste into your kitchen and dining room! When he ran out of waste, he apologized yet again and said "I'll see you soon!"

He returned with a huge smile, "You no longer have to wait for me, I figured out how to make sure I have an uninterrupted flow of waste to decorate your house with, I redirected all the sewer pipes from every house in the neighborhood and they are connected to the WWWW. Network."

You ask what do the four WWWW's stand for? And he responds "The **W**orld **W**ide **W**eb of **W**aste!

He explained "I connected the WWWW.CON to your sewer pipe so this way you will always have a constant sewer back-up and your hose will always be on to provide you with everyone else's waste!"

"When connected to the World Wide Web of Waste you never lack waste to pour into your home because you are connected to everybody else's waste!"

Your neighbor adds with excitement "there also exists *a national waste broadcasting stations* which collect the latest garbage. Not just your rubbish but also the waste of people locally and globally so you are always updated when people dump their waste on each other, and you get their waste almost in real time!"

Ask the students for their comments on the story and what they think the metaphor means?

Explain the Mashal:
Guide the students to identify the Nimshal, the meaning of the Mashal.

The waste coming out the hose are all the **negative thoughts**, anger, hate, resentment, thoughts of revenge appearing in your mind.

Your home is your mind!
Thoughts constantly knock on the door of your mind to let them in.[153]

Are you okay letting your neighbor into your house and hosing it down with human waste!???
Or other people's waste?
The whole entire world's waste?

Why not?

Why object? After all, it is all new waste. None of it is old waste, it is delivered to you in real time, or at least within minutes of the waste being spilled. It's available almost at the speed of light to be poured into your home! Aren't you excited by this innovative technology?!

The Torah instructs us in what to think and what not to think.

What is the danger of letting anybody into our home (our minds) and tell us their opinions?

What is the danger of listening to lots of people who are strangers tell us their reality?

Rambam writes how our surrounding culture and its values influence our behavior and attitudes. Precisely because of this reality, one needs to closely associate with Tzadikim and Chachamim whose actions and mind set will provide us the needed role models to combat the surrounding culture.

Rambam, Deos, Ch. 6. Halacha 1.
דרך ברייתו של אדם להיות נמשך בדעותיו ובמעשיו אחר ריעיו וחביריו נוהג כמנהג אנשי מדינתו, לפיכך צריך אדם להתחבר לצדיקים ולישב אצל החכמים תמיד

---

[153] See Likutei Moharan Volume I, Lesson 233 and Volume II, Lesson #51.

כדי שילמוד ממעשיהם, ויתרחק מן הרשעים ההולכים בחשך כדי שלא ילמוד ממעשיהם, הוא ששלמה אומר הולך את חכמים יחכם ורועה כסילים ירוע, ואומר אשרי האיש וגו', וכן אם היה במדינה שמנהגותיה רעים ואין אנשיה הולכים בדרך ישרה ילך למקום שאנשיה צדיקים ונוהגים בדרך טובים, ואם היו כל המדינות שהוא יודעם ושומע שמועתן נוהגים בדרך לא טובה כמו זמנינו, או שאינו יכול ללכת למדינה שמנהגותיה טובים מפני הגייסות או מפני החולי ישב לבדו יחידי כעניין שנאמר ישב בדד וידום, ואם היו רעים וחטאים שאין מניחים אותו לישב במדינה אלא אם כן נתערב עמהן ונוהג במנהגם הרע יצא למערות ולחוחים ולמדברות, ואל ינהיג עצמו בדרך חטאים כענין שנאמר מי יתנני במדבר מלון אורחים

If the students are sufficiently mature, you can learn with them the entire Hilchos Deos from the first Perek which describes in more detail the need to know what Hashem wants me to think in order to know how to act.

4.12 Metaphor #12: The Airport Carousel

Goal: What other people think is none of my business!

Story:
Once upon a time your plane arrived safely and now you are standing at baggage claim waiting for your suitcase to come around. Hundreds of pieces of luggage pass in front of you, but you know what your luggage looks like. So when other people's baggage passes by, do you pick it up? Or do you just acknowledge their existence BUT do not take it off the carousel and certainly don't take it home! You simply wait for your luggage to arrive!

But imagine you see someone elses baggage and instead of ignoring it, you take it off the carasol, open it up and go through all the contents! Then you close it and take it home!!

Ask the students to share what they think this may be a Mashol to?

Explanation:
Your thoughts are like pieces of luggage moving along a carasol. You do not have to pick up other people's baggage! Other people's reality is simply their reality! It is only their reality, period. It is never your reality.[154]

Other people's reality will never be your reality! It can never be exactly the same.[155]

You are designed perfect!
- You breath and exhale,
- You eat and expel,
- You think! And think, and then think a different thought, or you think and think and think! Thoughts come through your mind and disappear to be replaced by new thoughts.

But what if I catch a thought going around in my mind? For example, noticing a thought of pain, worry or fear coming through my mind and then I hold onto it, grab it, not letting go? What if I open this thought up and notice how it leads to other similar thoughts of pain, worry and fear?

---

[154] Except perhaps in a case where two witnesses give the identical testimony, in which case this is so rare that Bais Din accepts this as factual. If two people see something the exact same way, that creates a fact!
[155] Brachos 58a Ben Zoma would recite a blessing that celebrates how every person has a different mind - Baruch Chacham HaRazim.

Then I add other thoughts to prove that this fear *is* true, and I am justified to think these painful thoughts? What should I do?

- Find more proof for why this fear should be encouraged!?
- Ignore the thought?
- Distract myself?
- Tell myself "well! That's a thought! But only a thought! It does not have the power to make me have fear, unless I give it that power!"
- Turn the moment of fear into a Tefila - "Please Hashem, help me have more Emuna in You and not believe every thought I think.

So which one of the above should you select? And the answer is...*your choice*!

What if I truly think Mr. Ploni wronged me, and a thought of resentment toward Mr. Ploni enters my mind, but instead of deleting the thought, or allow it to disappear on its own, like the luggage moving passed me, I allow more thoughts of previous memories of when Mr. Ploni hurt me to join my present thought and now I am really upset!!

But the reason I am upset is because I am taking *other peoples words or actions and opening them up for inspection of their contents...* but it is only their reality!

It's their baggage! Not mine! Or perhaps more accurately stated - it is not even their reality but really *my thoughts of what I think they said or did* and intended!

So what is truly upsetting me?
Is Mr. Ploni really inside my mind?
How does he get inside my thoughts? Is that even possible?

Or is it *my thoughts I am thinking* about Mr. Ploni that are hurting me?

Everything that comes into my body is meant to be expelled:

My breath is inhaled and then exhaled and...

The waste in my food is expelled.

Even the nutrients in my food which become part of my trillions of cells turn into energy and eventually the cells die to be replaced with newly generated cells.

Nothing inside me stays exactly the same, because my body is renewing itself all the waking moments of my entire life!

If my body has a cut, it knows how to heal itself!

My body has the Divine Intelligence to know how to renew itself! How to regenerate itself! Even how to heal itself!

Why would thoughts of pain, fear, anxiety, depression, hate, resentment, anger or even revenge *belong inside me*? Is it possible we are designed to regenerate our minds?

Is it possible we are designed to heal our own painful thinking!? Is it possible that I am hurting myself with non-reality thinking?

Everything else is designed to exit if it cannot improve my health!

Only the nutritious elements in food become part of my body. Only the oxygen goes to my blood stream to bring energy to my 75 trillion cells while all the carbon dioxide is exhaled.

Toxicity in the food is expelled through sweat, urine and our bowel movement!

My body knows exactly how to identify what does not belong inside it, and rid itself of such waste.

So why would I hold onto *unhealthy thoughts inside my mind*, is that mentally healthy? Or is it **ILL** - LOGICAL!

No other part of my human anatomy is designed to hold onto what does not belong inside me, my body is in a constant state of renewal, cells die and are replaced with new cells.

So does it make any sense to hold onto thoughts that are hurting me?

Or is holding onto thoughts that don't belong inside me like taking other people's baggage, opening them up and taking them home!?

Should I rid myself of thoughts which hurt me? And if I do not ignore such thoughts going around the carousel of my mind, is that the beginning of me beating myself up? (see next Metaphor on beating myself up).

Ask the students what they are thinking in response to this metaphor?

Ask the students for any insights they have had since last week?

4.13 Metaphor #13:
Why would anyone repeatedly beat *themselves* up![156]

Goal:
Identify the true source of my feelings.
Experience the absurdity of repeated negative thoughts.

Step 1 - Tell this short story
Once upon a time, Mr. Ploni hit me with my own baseball bat, *"OUCH! I mean, that really hurt!"*
I have a bruise on the back of my head. I go home, and begin crying as soon as I see my Mum.
She asks: *"what happened?"*
I remove my baseball bat from my knapsack and I cry out "*Ploni hit me on the back of my head like this!*" And I proceed to hit myself with the bat in the exact same place and scream - *"OUCH! It really hurts, I hate him, he is so so mean!"*

Mum is catching her breath at the shock of me re-enacting the scene when Dad comes running upstairs from the basement office to find out what the painful screams are about.

I turn to Dad and with tears and hysterics, I again re-enact what Mr. Ploni did by hitting myself again with the bat!

My father pulls the bat away and urgently says *"we have to get you help."*

Dad calls his brother who is a therapist of repute who lives nearby and takes me immediately to my uncle's office in his house.

My uncle asks: what is the problem? I tell him the incident of Ploni hitting me with my baseball bat, and picking up the metal poker from my uncle's fire place I start crying as I burst into a renewed torrent of tears and cry out - *"Ploni hit me like this right here with my baseball bat"* and before my uncle can stop me, I have hit my head with the poker and am now in hysterical tears of pain.

Step 2
Ask the students for their insights into the Mashal and its Nimshal. Hints: What does the bat represent? Why am I re-enacting the incident? Why am I crying each time?

---

[156] This metaphor is adapted from the same heard from Dr. Dicken Bettinger, Practitioner of The Three Principles.

Ask the students to tell you what is wrong or disturbing about this story?

Ask the students why does it not help to pull the bat away from the boy?
(because the bat is thought in his mind hitting him and hurting him, so nobody can take the bat away, only himself!).
Some possible insights:
Each time I repeat the painful experience I actually bring the memory of pain into the moment, like bashing myself on the head again and again!

It appears that before the bruise on my head has had a chance to heal, I have hit myself again and re-opened the wound! Or worse, caused the bruise to become an open wound that can become infected!!

Step 3
Ask the students to tell you what they think is the meaning of the boy picking up the bat and hitting himself again each time he tells the story?
The repetition of the incident is my repeating my thoughts of what happened with all the associated pain.

So who exactly is hurting me when I repeat the incident to my Mum, Dad and Uncle?

The baseball bat is my thought! The repeated re-enactment is my beating myself up with thought in the moment!

What else could I do instead of repeating the pain? Let go!? But how?

The knowledge alone that only thought of the incident is what is paining me, allows to me to make a better choice when the painful memory pops up! **It's the knowledge that no person or experience can prevent you pressing delete that is the solution!**

There is nothing to actually do! It is more about my paying attention to where the thought is truly coming from that helps me know "what to do."

Nobody needs to give me a self-help book of how to drop the bat from my hand! I do not need to pay any professional to heal me because the 'to do' of this is so glaringly obvious and logical, I will let go of the bat as soon as I understand I am the one who is hitting myself with repeated painful memories!

If I believe the thought is coming from Ploni, I will remain in -
- 'I'm a victim' mode,
- 'I'm a target' mode,
- 'Pity me' mode or
- 'Save me' mode! Or
- 'Tell everyone how bad Ploni is' mode!

In my victim/target and Pity-Me Mode, I may even try to convince others to agree with how terrible ploni is and how victimized I have been! Before I know it, my very telling others of other peoples' crimes against me is what is reinforcing the very problem - **my obsessive thinking**!

I have fallen into the false belief that I have no control over my life and will not be safe till Ploni is dealt with! Or is out the way or leaves me alone.

BUT if I know the thought is coming from inside ME and I can explore it or ignore it, I am liberated from being chained to the 'outside-in' illusion!

If any student says they are having a hard time ignoring their thoughts repeatedly 'hitting' or 'popping-up' at them, then remind them that Hashem breathed into us His Essence, Tzelem Elokim, an Eternal Neshama, so we can always turn to Hashem. With that, ask the students if they remember the list we made (4.6 above) of Thank Yous we can say to Hashem? Here it is again:

1. "Thank you Hashem for the invitation to be silent to those who hurt me with words because now I can prove to You and myself how strong I am inside."
2. "Thank You Hashem for the bully because now I can turn to *You* instead of listening to my thoughts of fear, so the bully and my fear thoughts (Yetzer Hara) make me come closer to You."
3. "Thank You Hashem for the bully so I can get the Mitzvah of אמונה because I know everything comes from You because You love me. Now I will be stronger in my Emuna because of the bully!"
4. Thank You Hashem for the bully because now I can live the Mitzvah of being Davuk to You - ובו תדבק and another Mitzvah of בכל דרכיך דעהו, to be aware of You in every direction I go in.
5. "Thank You Hashem for bully because now I get the awesome Mitzvah of showing my love for You when I have thoughts of fear"[157]

---

[157] The Mitzvah to love Hashem is found in Dev. 6:5 - וְאָהַבְתָּ אֵת ה' אֱלֹקֶיךָ בְּכָל־לְבָבְךָ which Chazal tell us in Brachos 9:5 means to love Hashem with both your Yetzer Hara thoughts and Yetzer Tov thoughts - בִּשְׁנֵי יְצָרֶיךָ, בְּיֵצֶר טוֹב וּבְיֵצֶר רָע.

6. "Thank You Hashem for the bully because now I get the Mitzvah of not believing any other power exists except You![158] Because my Yetzer Hara makes me turn to You to save me instead of believing anything else can help me without Your help!"
7. In your next thought, you can **ask Hashem** "Please help me ignore both the bully and the fear I have of him."

Ask the students for any insights they have had since last week?

---

[158] This is the second Mitzvah in the Aseret HaDibros - Ex.20:3 - לֹא־יִהְיֶה לְךָ אֱלֹהִים אֲחֵרִים עַל־פָּנָי. Not to believe any other powers exist except Hashem.

4.14 Metaphor #14:
Would you carry a sack of other people's hammers to hit yourself?

Goal:
Understand how resentment is a thought in the moment and the Torah asks me to delete it.[159]

We achieve this goal with the following metaphor:
Remembering other people's mistakes is like carrying a sack of hammers and pulling one out at a time to hit myself!

Props:
- Plastic Hammers (or have kids cut out shape of hammers on hard card stock)
- Blank stickers.
- Bag or sack to put the hammers in.

Step 1.
Ask the students to each write a negative Midda or feeling on a sticker.

Step 2.
As you take a hammer out its bag, place one of the stickers on the handle and read the word on the sticker, e.g. *Anger* and say you are angry with Ploni[160] and why and bang yourself with the hammer on the head and cry "*Outch*!"

Pull out a second hammer read the second sticker as you place it on the handle, e.g. *Frustration*. And name another Ploni you are upset with and why you are frustrated.

Each time you pull out a hammer from the bag, describe a resentment you have against someone and bang yourself with the plastic hammer on the head and cry out "Outch!"

You want to dramatize the absurdity of hitting oneself with hammers, nobody would do such an insane act!

---

159 Lev. 19:18. וְלֹא־תִטֹּר אֶת־בְּנֵי עַמֶּךָ - See Rashi Yuma 23a. 'Netira' - 'remembering other people's mistakes against me' is this violation. It is done in thought, when I refuse to let go of such memories but continue to hang on to them, I am in violation of this Laav.
160 Ploni in English means an unnamed person, like the expression 'so and so' did such and such.

Step 3.
Ask the students: Does it make sense for anyone to carry a sack of hammers and keep taking them out and hitting themselves?
But is that not what I do when I think thoughts of resentment about how others treated me?

Step 4.
Ask the students to share what they learned from this Metaphor.

Encourage them to share an example of when they notice their own thoughts popping up and how this metaphor can help them visualize what they are doing to themselves when they repeatedly 'bang themselves' with resentful memories.

Background information

The following information is to help increase the leverage upon oneself to let go of resentful thoughts:
לא תטר - 'Don't carry a grudge' means do not remember other people's mistakes.

Rambam offers clarity on this Aveira: Instead of remembering what others did wrong and holding it against them, one should rather erase the matter from his mind and not hold onto such memories. As long as one holds onto the memory of their mistakes against you, and you continue to remember it, you are more likely to come to Nekama, revenge. That is why the Torah stresses the severity of thoughts of resentment. The Torah instructs us to literally erase their crime against us and not remember it at all! This is the correct attitude to adopt to allow people to get along with each other and conduct business together.

Rambam, Deos, 7:8

כל הנוטר לאחד מישראל עובר בלא תעשה שנאמר ולא תטר את בני עמיך, כיצד היא הנטירה? ראובן שאמר לשמעון השכיר לי בית זה או השאילני שור זה ולא רצה שמעון, לימים בא שמעון לראובן לשאול ממנו או לשכור ממנו ואמר לו ראובן הא לך הריני משאיל ואיני כמותך לא אשלם לך כמעשיך, העושה כזה עובר בלא תטר, **אלא ימחה הדבר מלבו ולא איטרנו, שכל זמן שהוא נוטר את הדבר וזוכרות שמא יבא לנקום**, לפיכך הקפידה תורה על הנטירה עד שימחה העון מלבו ולא זכרנו כלל, וזו היא הדעה הכונה שאפשר שתתקיים בה יישוב הארץ ומשאם ומתנם של בני אדם זה עם זה.

Yuma 23a

ואיזו היא נטירה? אמר לו: השאילני קרדומך - אמר ליה: לא. למחר אמר לו: השאילי חלוקך - אמר לו: הילך, איני כמותך, שלא השאלתני - זו היא נטירה.

What is Netira? Reuven asks Shimon "could you lend me your axe?" Shimon says "No!"
Later, Shimon asks Reuven to lend him a coat. Reuven says: "Sure, here it is, I am not like you, you refused to lend me (your axe). This is a classic case of Netira, baring a grudge, remembering what you think others did wrong to you.

Rashi (ibid)
איני כמותך שלא השאלתני זו היא נטירה - שהדבר שמור בלבו, ולא הסיחו מדעתו.

'The incident of Shimon (refusing to lend Reuven) has been preserved in his (Reuven's) mind and Reuven won't stop thinking about it.'

Rashi clearly understands the core of the Issur is that one is holding onto such thoughts and not removing them from his mind!

The Torah could not possibly ask me to let go of a memory if indeed it were not possible.

Nobody is exempt by saying "I cannot forget what that person did to me!" And if indeed the memory of that misdeed against me does 'pop up,' Hashem wants me to press delete! Let go of the thought.

Note that the context of this Mitzvah of Netira is in the very same Passuk[161] as Nekama and Ahavas Yisrael, all three items are *thought in the moment,* to demonstrate how Hashem gives us a vote of confidence that we really can move from one thought to the next. Hashem even signs off His Name at the end of the Passuk as if to say "I know you can delete the thoughts of revenge and resentment, and go to a thought of love for that person, because I am the One Who designed you!

Ask the students for any insights they have had since last week?

---

[161] לֹא־תִקֹּם וְלֹא־תִטֹּר אֶת־בְּנֵי עַמֶּךָ וְאָהַבְתָּ לְרֵעֲךָ כָּמוֹךָ אֲנִי ה'

4.15 Metaphor #15:
Carrying a sack of painful memories wherever I go!

Goal:
To dramatize the absurdity of carrying the burden of negative thoughts and repeating them again and again.

Props:
- Stones or small rocks collected from outside.
- Bag or sack to hold the rocks.
- Blank stickers for students to write on.
- Rubber bands.

Step 1.
Give one sticker to each student.
Give one rock to each student.
Ask the students to write an unhappy thought or feeling on their sticker and then stick or rubber band it to their rock and bring it to the front of the class and place it in the bag/sack.

Step 2.
Dramatize carrying the sack of rocks, walking back and forth in front of the class, and complain about the weight of this load. Then open up the sack and begin reading each sticker with exaggerated pain and groaning.

Each rock is a memory (thought) in the moment of what I resent about other people or my life.

After you read all the stickers on the rocks, return them to the sack and put it back on your back and continue walking to and fro in front of the class moaning, groaning and complaining about how much weight you are carrying in your life!

Ask the students for any insights they have had since last week?

4.16 Metaphor #16:
Returning one's hand to the burning stove!

Goal:
Experience the freedom that you can think any thought you want! Any time you want, in any circumstance!

Non-Reality Thinking is like **burning one's hand on the stove** and then returning to touch the stove again! That's crazy, insane!

Reality Thinking means we can stop our hand from returning to the stove, we can stop thinking painful thoughts by going to the next thought!

Story:
Once upon a time, Mr. Ploni heated the ring on his stove to boil water in a pot. By mistake, he touched the ring when it was burning hot and burnt his hand rather badly. He then went back to the stove to touch it again! And then again! Everyone agrees, nobody would do that unless they are mentally insane! (I doubt even a mentally insane person would do that either!)

Lesson:
Invite the students to share their insights

Explain:
We are all born with mental health.
We are all sitting in the middle of mental health, we just forget it or don't know it!
We all agree that burning ourselves one time should be the last time we ever put our hand near a hot stove again. So why do we keep remembering the people and times we were burnt by other people's insults and unkind actions?

If each time we remember what they did to us, we would feel pain, how is that different from putting my hand back on the stove?

Why would I let my thoughts return to the memories of being burnt by others?

The good news is we are always only one thought away from the next thought, so how hard is it for me to remove my hand, my thought from the memory of being burned?
We are always one thought away!

We are always one thought away from mental well-being!

And what is mental wellbeing?

Gratitude to Hashem for His endless blessings - that is mental wellbeing!

So as soon heavy thoughts of anger, resentment and bitterness of yesterday pop up in your mind, immediately turn to Hashem with your thank You list:

Thank You Hashem for my resentful thoughts because now I can show my love for You by ignoring them!

Thank You Hashem for my anger thoughts because now I can prove my love for You by turning my Yetzer Hara into praise and gratitude to You.

Thank You Hashem for inviting me to turn to You with Tefila each time I get a pop-up thought that is not a reality thought.

Ask the students for any insights they have learned since last week?

4.17 Metaphor #17: Internal Windshield Wipers

Goal:
Increased awareness that:
I can wipe away unpleasant thoughts.

Story/Mashal:
Once upon a time, you were driving in heavy rain and the wet roads were also muddy. The car in front of you kept kicking up both rain and mud onto your windshield.
You turned on your windshield wipers to wipe off the rain and muddy water. Even though one second later, more rain and muddy water sprayed onto your windshield, you simply kept the wipers on.

Nimshal/Meaning of the Mashal:
We all have thoughts passing through our minds. Sometimes they are *muddy* thoughts *raining* down on us from what people say or do. Or things happen to us that we do not like. It feels like *mud* is being *rained* upon us!

Do we keep the mud on the windows of our mind or does every one of us have Internal Windshield Wipers constantly able to wipe off dirty mud being kicked up by the wheels of the car in front of you (other peoples negative behavior)?[162]

You always have the innate health inside you all the time to handle mud that is thrown at you! Just like the windshield wipers come with the body of the car (so you can see clearly even when it's raining and muddy water hits your screen), so too, your mind came with its own *internal wipers* to wipe off insults, unkind words and even unhappy memories.

But, there is one thing you must do! Turn on the wipers!

So where is the switch in your mind to turn on your internal wipers?

The answer is so simple! **The 'on' switch is in your next thought!**

---

[162] You could extend the meaning of the metaphor. The car in front of you is not deliberately trying to make your vision blurry by mudding your windshield. The car in front is going on its own path to get to where it is going. When it rains and the roads are muddy, this is simply what happens, your windshield will be muddied from the mud kicked up from the car in front of you. So too, life has its rainy moments, and when it is hard, it may actually be hard for the guy in front of you too! He is getting rid of rain and mud in his way, but not to hurt you, that is just his reality, his path and he is going through life just like you are!

Without the wipers on, you will not be able to see the road clearly and might make a poor decision!

The road of life ahead of you may be murky and unclear from all the unhappy thoughts and non-reality thinking, then we are more likely to make poor decisions!

But the good news is that no matter how much rain or mud falls on the windows of your mind, you are always one thought away from wiping away the mud!

What will be your next thought?

Any thought you choose! But the best thoughts to have are praise and gratitude to Hashem for the rain and mud!

When you thank Hashem for the rain and mud, you are turning on your internal windshield wipers. Your innate wisdom, your innate Neshama is always inside you because Hashem is inside you powering your mind and body, so He is so very close by.

The Torah[163] itself says so:

כִּי־קָרוֹב אֵלֶיךָ הַדָּבָר מְאֹד בְּפִיךָ וּבִלְבָבְךָ לַעֲשֹׂתוֹ

It is exceedingly close to you to do because it is in your mouth and thoughts to do it!

Just say sorry!
Just say Thank You Hashem!
Just say I love You Hashem!

---

[163] Dev. 30:14. The Passuk is referencing the Mitzvah of Teshuva and declaring that it is a very easy Mitzvah, so exceedingly close to you because it is in your mouth and thoughts to do it (Teshuva). A הרהור תשובה literally means a 'changed thought.'

4.18 Metaphor #18:
A Man with Pneumonia keeps sneezing & coughing in other people's faces!

Goal:
Know you have the power to shut out non-reality thoughts and other people's negative opinions.

Story/Mashal:
Once upon a time, you were sitting with a number of other people in a waiting room and a gentleman with a terrible cough walks into the same room as you. He goes from person to person and sneezes and coughs right into their faces!

How outraged we would all be in seeing him cough his germs directly into people's faces!

Ask the students which do they think is worse?

Coughing in another person's face and dumping their germs on them or

Dumping complaints, Lashon Hara and Onas Devarim in the ears of people around them?

Ask the students to comment on the metaphor of sneezing and coughing being parallel to other people dumping their Non-Reality-Thinking on you!

Ask the students to comment on the following:
What if you saw someone coughing and sneezing into a special container that holds all the germs he just coughed and sneezed. Then you see him take a deep breath and inhale the germs from the container back into his lungs!

Is he acting logically or **ILL**-Logically?

The point being: Do we not do the same when we *re-think* Non-Reality Thoughts? Are we not also inhaling the germs in our minds each time we hold onto such thoughts? Re-inhaling unhealthy thoughts is what is making us ill!

Ask the students for any insights they have had since last week?

4.19 Metaphor #19:
Select your own weather!
You were born with your own internal weather system!

Goal: You always have the power to change your internal weather from storm to sunny!

Consider -
Have you ever been out to recess in the freezing cold? Or when it's raining? But you were so focused on the game you were playing that the weather did not really matter? Why not?

Because you were not *paying attention* to it. Your *mind* was on the game!

Have you ever been on a trip or a walk with a friend and it was cloudy, overcast, or raining, yet because you really enjoyed the company of the person with you, your best friend or favorite cousin, you simply *paid no attention* to the weather?

So can the weather really make us happy or sad? Or is it what *I THINK* that makes me feel happy or sad?

You *think* it is raining or is it's sunny **depending on *whatever weather you decide - inside*!**

If you are with your best friend or your fiancé/groom or Kalah, the weather is barely noticeable because you are with your best friend or fiance, so nothing else matters! You are not paying attention to the weather outside because your attention is on the *internal weather*! What you are thinking! You are focused on your friend or fiancé!

Point to Consider -
What if a Tzadik felt that way about always knowing Hashem is with him or her wherever he/she goes!?[164] Meaning, he is never alone because The One Who loves him the most, Hashem, is right with him always! So it is always sunny!

Some say, if you love what you do, you don't have to ever work a day in your life!

---

164 See Shulchan Aruch, Orach Chaim, Siman #222.3 for the reason why Ovdei Hashem can find simcha even when adversity strikes. Also see Siman #231 which describes how one can serve Hashem all the time, no matter what we are doing, because the true us is our thought in the moment.

This is a similar idea to our metaphor of *internal weather*, when a person truly loves his work, it is not a burden to him. As Chazal say (Avot. 1:10) שְׁמַעְיָה אוֹמֵר, אֱהוֹב אֶת הַמְּלָאכָה

So too, a טוב לב, a good mind, is at a משתה תמיד, a constant banquet. It is not what is going on outside that makes the true difference between happy and unhappy, it is always what is going on inside that is the ONLY measure of reality!

4.20 Metaphor #20:
"I'll Do It My Waze!" You come with your own GPS system

Goal:
You are never lost! You can always rely on your internal GPS system to guide you.

GPS stands for **G**-d's **P**ositioning **S**ystem! And *it is always on* - no matter how lost you are, it is always redirecting you! (If you will but listen to its directions!)

Non-Reality Thinking covers the sound of your Neshama/Innate health, but your internal GPS is always guiding you.[165]

If you cannot hear your GPS, what should you do?
1. Know it is always on.
2. Ask Hashem to direct you & wait!
3. Thank Hashem you are lost! And ask Him to redirect you!

Point to consider -
Every morning we agree Hashem is guiding our every footstep -

בָּרוּךְ אַתָּה יְיָ אֱלֹקֵינוּ מֶלֶךְ הָעוֹלָם, הַמֵּכִין מִצְעֲדֵי גֶבֶר

When you say this Bracha each morning, this is a good place to ask Hashem "*Wherever I go today, please guide me to the right place at the right time*" and then trust His GPS is on inside you!

Practical Advice:
Sefarim give excellent advice to train yourself to ask Hashem every morning as soon as you finish Modeh Ani, *"Please guide me today so that everything I do, say and think only be according to Your Ratzon, and anyone dependent upon me."*

This Tefila comes from Rabbi Nachman of Breslov who encouraged one to start one's day this way so that need not worry or be upset by any thoughts of anxiety the remainder of the day since one already threw oneself on Hashem saying that I want to do whatever is *His* will.[166]

Ask the students for any insights they have had since last week?

---

[165] See Sichot HaRan, Paragraph #7. When a person has a confusing thought, Hashem will send him a thought that will untangle his confusion. See also Likutey Moharan I, Lesson #137 and #138.
[166] Sichos HaRan, Paragraph #2. Also see Sichos HaRan, #238 which offers similar advice when saying the words in the Evening Tefila - ותקננו מלכנו בעצה טובה מלפניך to guide us to only think, say and do only whatever Hashem wants from us over the next 24 hours.

4.21 Metaphor #21: Phew! It was only a dream!

Goal:
Remind myself that no matter how painful my past memories are, now they are only thought. I am never relegated to a second class experience of life because of yesterdays' memories.

Story:
Once upon a time, you woke up in sweat after a frightening dream![167]

Why are you so relieved within one second after you awaken from a nightmare? Oh! Because you realize *it was not real*.

Neither is *yesterday's* pain real *now*, because yesterday's pain is now history, it is not here in the now - unless you bring the memory into the moment and try relive it! But it is still only a memory. Not real, not happening to you now.

The nightmare was only real till you woke up! Now you know it's gone, you are no longer living in it. There is nothing to fear.

Ask the students -
What can we learn from this metaphor of all past memories that are unpleasant being like an unpleasant dream?

Point to consider -
According to Chazal, the biggest wakeup call is death! That is when we will see how much we slept this world away with foolish fears, worries, anxiety, etc.[168]

Ask the students for any insights they have had since last week?

---

[167] "It was a good dream, it was a good dream, it was a good dream!"
[168] Sichos HaRan, Paragraph #83. See also Targum on Koheles 12:13. That when we die, all we ever did, said and thought will be 'heard' by all, meaning, all the people who lived before us will see our life played back to us. What an embarrassment to see all the thoughts I wasted on Non-Reality!

4.22 Metaphor #22: The Sun is always shining! True or False?

Ask the students:
- Have you ever been on a plane?
- When you were flying above the clouds, was it ever raining?
- Why did it not rain above the clouds?

Because there is no rain above the clouds! No hail, snow or sleet above the clouds.

Hey! The sun is always shining above the clouds![169]

True or false:
The sun is always shining outside planet earth - True or False?[170]

The bigger the context of your reality, the more sunshine you let in!

The more you ignore the *cloudy thoughts*, the more the sun shines inside you!
How far away are you from letting the sunshine in?

Always only One thought away!

Ask the students what their thoughts are on this metaphor.

The metaphor can be seen as **Hashem's Light always shining in our lives**. When we let it shine inside out, we have no fear of anything other than awe for Hashem. As David HaMelech declared[171] -
"Hashem, You are my Light & salvation, so from who I should fear?"

When the **Kotzke Rebbe** z"l was challenged "where is G-d?"
He replied "Wherever you let Him in!"
Meaning, Hashem is everywhere all the time.
The light of His constant love for us is always shinning.
Whenever we let Him in, He is immediately there because the point of entry is our 'thought' so the moment we think of Him, He is there.
The light of the Menora in the Bais Hamikdash lit up the entire Heichal and the slit windows of the Heichal on the inside and the broad opening of the same windows on the outside meant that the light was exuding from inside out. We always have Hashem's light shining inside us.

Ask the students for any insights they had since last week?

---

[169] True, the sun is always shining above the clouds except when your side of the earth is not facing the sun!

[170] True, so long as the moon does not eclipse the sun!

[171] Tehilim 27:1 - לְדָוִד ה' אוֹרִי וְיִשְׁעִי מִמִּי אִירָא

4.23 Metaphor #23: Imagine your car has two steering wheels![172]

Goal:
See how the Yetzer Hara is a thought, and so is my Yetzer HaTov a thought, and though they seem to fight over my mind, I can always choose which thought will win.

Story:
Once upon a time you are driving a very strange car. It has two sets steering wheels! One in the driver's seat and the other in the front passenger seat!

Your car also has two sets of breaks and two gas pedals!

You just assume it is an unusual design, till you discover the passenger next to you can actually turn the car in a different direction than you want to go in! But there is both good and bad news, which do you want to hear first?

The good news is you are behind the wheel which always overrides the driver in the other seat!

The bad news is if you don't take control of steering in the direction you want to go in, the other driver will drive you away from your destination, or even get you lost!

The two steering wheels are the Yetzer Hatov and Yetzer Hara[173] - your good thoughts and your not good thoughts. Or as we have been calling them, Reality Thoughts and Non-Reality Thoughts.

For a more dramatic effect, you can act out driving in one direction, and pretend the car goes in another direction the moment you let go of your steering wheel.

Ask the students - how far are you away from taking back control of the car? One thought away!

Ask the students for any insights they have had since last week?

---

[172] I read this metaphor from Aviva Barnett's website mindworks.com, she is an iHeart practitioner.
[173] Likutey Moharan. I. Lesson #49 describes the Yetzer Tov as the מחשבות טובות and the Yetzer Hara as the מחשבות רעות.

4.24 Metaphor #24:
The Horse & Rider Metaphor[174] - Who is taking who for a ride?

Goal:
To remember the truth is always the truth, you can choose the next thought. You always have control over the next thought.

Story:
Once upon a time you see in the distance a man riding a horse. You then wonder in your mind 'who is taking who for a ride?'

You then ask yourself, "Is it true the horse can turn in a different direction than its rider wants to go in?"

"Hmmm, you then ask "How much effort does the rider need to turn the horse back to where the rider wants to go?"

You answer your own question: The rider has the reins in his hands and with the smallest of movements can turn the horse back on the route the rider wants to go in.

Ask the students:
- **Who is the Rider?** You are the Rider.
- **Who is the horse?** Your thoughts are the horse!
- **What are the horse reins?** The reins are *your power* to divert your next thought to any direction you want to take your thoughts.

Your thoughts are always in your hands to direct wherever you decide to focus.
They are always in the power of the person to turn them away from wherever they take him and he can redirect them with hardly any effort. Because he is always one thought away from a different thought.

How long will the horse take you away from where you want to go? As long as you let him!
So, how far away are you from moving the horse back to where you want to go? One thought away!

Ask the students for their comments on this metaphor.

Ask the students for any insights they have had since last week?

---

[174] This metaphor is found in Likutey Moharan II Lesson #50. Rav Nachman offers that the metaphor of a rider and a horse is parallel to a person and his thoughts. Just like the rider can turn the horse in any direction he wants with a very slight effort and movement of the reins, so too, a person always has the power to turn his mind to anything he wants to focus on, always!

4.25 Metaphor #25:
Rain drops are falling on my head!
A leaking roof is flooding your home!

Goal:
You can always fix the leaks of negative thoughts leaking into your mind.

Story:
Once upon a time, there is a terrible rain storm outside, so you decide to relax on your couch and and read your favorite story book and suddenly drops of water fall on your head.

Oy vey! The roof is leaking! If it is not stopped the rain water will flood your house, cause dampness and mold which can lead to destruction of furnishings, valuable possessions and become a health hazard to boot! And still worse, delays you finishing your book!

Why is your roof built with a slant?
Obviously rain water will fall off into the gutters which then direct the rain water away from your house. But when there is a leak....Oy Vey!

Ask the students -
Can you stop the rain? No, of course not!
Can you fix the roof?

*You **cannot** stop the rain....but you **can** fix the roof!*

Ask the students -
- What are gutters for?
- What do the gutters do with the water?
- Direct the water away from the house.
- What is the rain a metaphor for?
- What is your house a metaphor for?

The rain is like thought. You cannot stop the rain, you cannot stop thoughts popping inside your mind.

The house is your mind.

Rain is not bad, it is indeed a blessing. But not if it is leaking inside your home!
Not if it floods your home and damages your possessions!

Thought does not have to be bad, it is thought.
But can Non-Reality Thoughts cause damage to your mind?

If you do not stop the leaking of Non-Reality Thoughts, how will it influence your character?
Thoughts that hurt are invitations to delete them and move onto the next thought.

Ask the children to expand on the metaphor, ask them if your mind has gutters? Ask what are the gutters of your mind which direct non-reality thoughts away from your attention?

If the children have a hard time expanding on the metaphor, you can offer the following to more fully flesh out the metaphor:
Did Hashem design your mind *not* to let in insults or unkind words?
Can you stop life from any harm that may 'rain' down on you?
Can you stop what happens to you? Not really, but can you decide what to let stay in or on your mind and what not to let in or stay?

If thoughts rain inside your mind and they are unhappy thoughts, stressful thoughts and they begin flooding your mind, can you fix your roof? How quick can you fix it?

Your house has gutters to redirect the rain away from the house! What are the gutters of your mind?

The answer is, *your next thought are the gutters of your mind!* You can actually turn the gutter into your house or away from it!

We are created by Hashem to have internal gutters to rid ourselves of toxicity.
For example:
Our skin expels toxicity through our sweat glands,[175]
Our lungs exhale carbon dioxide.
Our bowels digest and then expel toxic waste through the urine and anus.
Our Mind also has a sewage system to remove toxic thought.

THOUGHT in the MOMENT is your internal gutter for all waste!

---

[175] That's why exercise is so important, it accelerates the expulsion of acidity in our body through the lymph system.

It is so simple that we don't pay attention to thought in the moment and its power to expel toxic thoughts.

Similar to air being around us all the time, we hardly pay attention to it! Despite it being our life line!

Thought is so obviously 100% of our entire life experience, we hardly pay attention to it. Despite it being the source of our life experience and emotions!

It's like asking a fish - "how is the water?" And the fish looks all around him and responds "Water! What water?"
He does not see it, though he lives inside it!

We do not see air, though we breath it every moment of our waking lives.

We do not see thought, though we can only experience all of life inside thought!

Hashem created emotions so we could know what we are thinking. Our emotions are arrows which point to the origin of that emotion, thought in that moment!

Ask the students to comment on this idea that we live inside thought all the time.

Ask the students for any insights they have had since last week?

4.26 Metaphor #26:
The King Hired His General to Stir a Rebellion![176]

Goal:
1. Increase awareness that the Yetzer Hara was created to be ignored!
2. To explain what does serving Hashem with both the Yetzer HaTov and the Yetzer Hara mean?[177]

Story:
Once upon a time there was a king. He was very kind and generous to the people in his kingdom. The king was very wise and decided on a plan to know who in his kingdom are loyal to him and who are not.

The king called for a secret meeting with the general of his army and told him his plan. He commanded the general to take an entire battalion of soldiers from the king's army and go to every town in the kingdom. At the gates of every town the general would send a message to the leader of the town that the general has come with his army to invite the leader and all his town to rebel against the king!

If the town agrees to join the rebellion, then the general will not harm the town. But if the town refuses to join the rebellion, the general will come back later with his army and lay siege till they surrender.

The king explained that his plan was not to actually destroy any of his towns at all, only to reveal who is loyal to the king and who is not.

The general took his soldiers and went from town to town. Most towns refused to join the rebellion against the king, they loved their king who was only good and kind to them. They told the general to leave them alone and if he brings his soldiers back to fight, the town will fight the general and his army but will not surrender or join his rebellion against their beloved king.

Some towns were too afraid to fight the general and the sight of his army made them weaken their loyalty to the king and they agreed to join the rebellion. The general would then tell them he will inform them when the rebellion will take place.

---

176 This Metaphor is based on Medrash Mishley. Mashal #1
177 Mishna Brachos 9:5.

In one town there was a Tzadik and Chacham, a very righteous and wise man. When he received the message from the general, he realized straight away that something did not make any sense.

How could the general of the king get away with traveling across the country and threatening each town to join his rebellion against the king without the king knowing about this planned rebellion?

The Chacham realized this had to be a set up. It was just a plan to find out who was loyal and who was weak in their loyalty to the king. The Chacham left the town gates and went straight to the general and told him: "I know exactly why you have come, you are not rebelling against the king at all, in fact, you have been sent by the very king himself!"

"You simply want to find out who is really loyal to him and who is not. So I am telling you now, don't bother threatening us, we know the threat is not real, it is all an illusion. Leave us alone, we would never rebel against the king!"

The general was so happy to hear the Chacham's words because really there is no enemy of the king, the entire threat is just a camouflage to reveal who loves the king and who is not loyal.

Questions for the students:
1. Who is the king in this metaphor? (Hashem)
2. Who is the general? (The Yetzer Hara)
3. Who is the Chacham? (The Tzadikim in every generation)
4. Ask them to explain their understanding of the metaphor.

For example:
According to this story, is the general, the Yetzer Hara really our enemy?
Or is he a messenger from the King, Hashem Himself, to invite me to show me my inside metal? My inner strength?
Who is the real me inside me?
I am thought. I also have a Neshama which gives me the power to think and be aware of my thoughts.

When I think about how much Hashem does for me, I feel love and loyalty to Hashem - The True King.

How do I fight the Yetzer Hara? By ignoring it!

Because the Yetzer Hara is thought in the moment! We win by not fighting, we win by ignoring it,[178] we win by knowing -

Hashem wants me to serve Him with my Yetzer Hara by not listening to it!

Platform for more discussion -
The Yetzer Hara is our מחשבות רעות.[179]
We are not commanded anywhere in Taryag Mitzvos *not* to have a Yetzer Hara!
We are commanded to not listen to it!
We are commanded to not pay attention to it![180]
We are commanded to ignore it!
We are commanded to cut out the 'pop-up' thoughts of the Yetzer Hara.[181]

Just like your teeth, if you ignore them, they will go away!
Just like a bully who does not get power from you because you give no space in your mind to him, he will go elsewhere.

The Yetzer Hara is a creation of Hashem with a holy mission - to be ignored!

Likutey Eitzos & the Sh'lah HaKadosh. Shaar HaOtiot
אין האדם מצֻוֶה שלא יהיה לו יצר הרע !
אלא שלא ישמע לו

היצר הרע הוא 'נברא' של השם ית'
והוא נברא במטרה קדושה - שלא נשמע לו !

Translation - We are not commanded not to have a Yetzer Hara! We are commanded not to listen to it. The Yetzer Hara was created by Hashem with the special mission to invite us not to listen to it! When Hashem commands us in Kriat Shema to love Him with all our לבבכם, *all our thoughts*. It means with both the Yetzer Tov and Yetzer Hara. As explained in the Mishna Brachos 9:5 -

---

178 Likutey Moharan, II, Lesson 51.
179 Likutey Moharan I, Lesson #49.
180 Num. 15:39 - וְלֹא תָתוּרוּ אַחֲרֵי לְבַבְכֶם
181 Dev. 10:15 - וּמַלְתֶּם אֵת עָרְלַת לְבַבְכֶם. 'Orlat HaLev' refers to the mind being 'blocked.' 'Blocked' from what? From thinking with clarity, from Reality-Thoughts (see Rashi Ex.6:12). Non-Reality thoughts are the Yetzer Hara which is called Orla (Sukka 52a) and blocks our mind from seeing Hashem is always with us all the time waiting for us to see Him and His unlimited kindness to us. See Rashi Ex. 17:2 - תָּמִיד אֲנִי בֵּינֵיכֶם וּמְזֻמָּן לְכָל צָרְכֵיכֶם, וְאַתֶּם אוֹמְרִים "הֲיֵשׁ ה' בְּקִרְבֵּנוּ אִם אָיִן"

חַיָּב אָדָם לְבָרֵךְ עַל הָרָעָה כְּשֵׁם שֶׁהוּא מְבָרֵךְ עַל הַטּוֹבָה, שֶׁנֶּאֱמַר (דברים ו:ה) וְאָהַבְתָּ אֵת יְיָ אֱלֹקֶיךָ בְּכָל לְבָבְךָ וּבְכָל נַפְשְׁךָ וּבְכָל מְאֹדֶךָ. **בְּכָל לְבָבְךָ, בִּשְׁנֵי יְצָרֶיךָ, בְּיֵצֶר טוֹב וּבְיֵצֶר רָע.**

We have explained that the Yetzer Hara is thought in the moment, so this metaphor of the King & His general was selected to teach how do we love Hashem with the Yetzer Hara? By ignoring it! And that is called loving Hashem! Ignore the general, no matter how impressive he is, he is only inviting me to show my love and loyalty to Hashem by not listening to the him! And don't forget, the general is himself a messenger of The King!

4.27 Metaphor #27:
Latest Touch Screen Technology - The METS Watch - 'Mind-Emotion-Touch-Screen.'

Goal:
Remind ourselves how our feelings are 100% what we are thinking in that moment.

Tell the students this imaginative scenario and then follow the practical steps below:

Story in the future.
Once upon the future, technology was so advanced, it invented a wireless touch-screen, about the size of your wrist watch. This screen is wirelessly connected to your thoughts and feelings! The scientists who invented it call it the METS watch. The word **METS** stands for **M**ind-**E**motion-**T**ouch-**S**creen. It is called the METS Watch because it is worn on your wrist like a watch and is the size of a small wrist watch.

The front screen has a letter **H** facing you and the letter **D** on the other side against your skin.
If you touch the H on one side of the screen, every **H**appy thought you ever experienced floods your memory! Every kind word, compliment, from the time you were born till now enters your mind! You feel on top of the world, you are so happy when you touch the H side of your touch screen that you never want to remove your finger from it!

Touch the other side of the screen with the **D**, then every **D**epressing thought, painful memory, experience, unkind word, insult, anguish, humiliation enters your mind! You soon feel so down and depressed that you begin to think you will never get out of feeling so so down. To touch the D screen, you have to remove the METZ Watch from your wrist and then touch the screen.

The amazing thing about this technology is that whenever you are having a hard day, or difficult moment or you feel overwhelmed, all you need do to remind yourself about how much good there really is in your life is simply touch the H button and you are instantly reminded of all the good you have ever experienced and in a moment you begin feeling so grateful to Hashem for all the blessings in your life.

Ask the students:
Would you give this technology to your friends, your brother, your mother or father? *Why not?*
If you give it to anyone else, they will have complete control over your thoughts and emotions!

Ask yourself:
Would you give this technology to your mother-in-law?
To your spouse, to your teenager?
To your boss?

Of course NOT!

Why would you <u>not</u> let anybody come close to this technology?
Why would you guard your METS Watch very closely?
Why is there nobody you would trust to take over your mind and emotions?

These guided questions are meant to elicit responses in your students which show they have understood the Metaphor. The message is that not only would you never let others access your Mind-Emotion Touch Screen, but much more than that - nobody ever can access it because both buttons are inside you, nobody can ever access it!

So do your best to insure your students are articulating the nonsense of ever believing anything outside of me can ever control what I think or feel. I am the only one who can ever access this technology, because it is my thought, nobody else's, which generates my feelings and experience.

Practical Application of this:
Step 1.
A. Ask the students to split into pairs.
B. Each student then cuts out a piece of card the size of watch face and write his/her initials at the top of their card.
C. Each student then writes the letter **H** on one side and **D** on the other.
  We will call this the *METS Watch* (**M**ind-**E**motion **T**ouch **S**creen).
D. Ask each student to exchange their **METS** Watch with their partner.

Step 2.
Each partner takes turns in answering the question "why should I give you back your METS Watch?" And the partner has to give as many reasons why he/she does not want anybody controlling his mind and emotions.

Step 3.
Ask the students to share their feedback (their reasons they gave each other to return their METS Watch).

Ask them to share any thoughts or insights they had.

Step 4. The Revelation!
Ask them "*Is it ever possible for anyone to actually take your METS Watch away from you? Ever!*"

By this question you want the students to explore the REALITY THINKING of

Knowing nobody ever can press your D button, ever!

Because it is SAFE INSIDE YOU all the time!

Clearly, you would not want anyone to have that amount of control over you!

So why do we sometimes say to ourselves that "so and so makes me so mad?" "This person is causing me so much stress!"
"Ploni drives me crazy!"
Is that not as though I have given others the power to press whichever side of the screen they choose!?
Again, it is not as though we will never experience anger or frustration or pain ever again. This world is a constant Olam Hanissayon. It is simply knowing the true source of our anger and frustration that helps us recognize Hashem hiding behind the 'general' (in metaphor #26 above) inviting me to rebel against the king. It's Hashem hiding behind the 'provocation' to anger or disappointment to *invite* me to reveal me internal strength.

Hashem is inviting me to decide what will be my next thought, delete or explore!?

Ask the students for any insights since last week.

4.28 Metaphor #28:
How High-Tech Advertising is a Metaphor for
How Hashem runs the world!

One of the biggest challenges we all face is how to make sense from the seemingly poor results for our hard efforts. We make so much effort to overcome our yetzer hara, change bad habits. But sometimes we might feel Hashem is not helping us enough to overcome them (הס ושלום). How much do I have to keep trying?

The Goal of the following metaphor is to understand where the Yetzer has the power to keep coming back and how to cut off that power!
This 'cut off' will help us understand what it takes to overcome bad habits![182]

Today's advertising is so sophisticated. Technology can track your exact spending habits and create a very accurate profile of your likes and dislikes so the advertising company know how to target you with what you will most likely want to buy. How exactly this works will be explained in more detail soon.

The Chafetz Chaim wrote that one of the reasons for the accelerated growth of technology before Mashiach is in order to make it more easy to have Emuna in Hashem and His Perfect Hashgacha Pratit, supervision of the world.

Concepts expressed in Chazal 2,000 years ago as metaphors are today an everyday reality.

Chazal wrote 2,000 years ago that there is a seeing eye and hearing ear and everything we do is recorded.[183] Two thousand years ago, you needed simple Emuna in such a claim. Today, that Emuna is experienced every day! We have recordings of every phone call, almost every street corner, store and school have security cameras scanning almost every inch of the room and streets; the names, addresses and phone numbers of every person in the USA can fit onto a single USB memory stick, easily!

---

182 Additional goals of this metaphor are 1. To see how all technology is a metaphor to make Emuna in Hashem easy. And 2. See how everything we think really does make a difference in our life.
183 Avot. 2:1

In very recent years, the advertising industry has achieved new levels of sales. By using technology to collect very specific information about customers, they can use algorithms, a specific set of rules and steps to determine a solution, in this case to solve how to identify the most likely products the customer will buy. It is called Targeted Advertising. They build profiles of customers based on their spending habits, taste in clothing, shoes, books, foods, movies, sports, entertainment, how much they pay how often they buy, etc,.

Advertisers identify specific patterns of buying. Every purchase we make is being recorded in data bases which advertising companies access and then identify precise buying patterns to enable them to automatically pop-up the type of products we are most likely to buy! These pop-up ads are found on phones with screens and every time you buy on-line.

*The information **we are feeding** from our very own buying patterns* allow the advertisers to infer the probabilities of customers liking a product category. Utilizing such information, they construct a targeted advertising system and bombard us with suggestions that match our buying behaviors. Amazon does this all the time, so does Netflix in collecting favorite types of movies.

So how is the new world of advertising helping us understand how Hashem runs the world?

We can use the understanding of *Targeted advertising* to bring a totally new level of *Emuna in Chazal*!

And that is how Chazal inform us of how Hashem works *Midda Keneged Midda*.[184]

Hashem runs the world according the precise measure of our output.[185]
Shimshon HaGibor followed his eyes, so he lost his eyesight.
Miriam waited to see what would happen to baby Moshe and all Klal Yisrael had to wait for her recovery from Tzaraas.
Hashem pays us back measure for measure, Midda Keneged Midda.

The Gemora[186] has a statement that helps us understand how Hashem decides how to pay us Midda Keneged Midda - בדרך שאדם רוצה לילך בה, מוליכין אותו

---

184 Mishna, Sota 1:7, 8 & 9.
185 See the Mishnayos Sota, 1:7-9 for many examples.

The correct translation is - '*in the direction a person wants to go, **they** accompany him.*'

The Marasha[187] says the wording should read - '*In the direction a person wants to go in (singular) he is led.*' (יוֹלִךְ אוֹתוֹ).

Why does it switch to plural in the second half of the sentence and write '***they** accompany him*' (מוֹלִיכִין אוֹתוֹ)?
Who is '**they?**'

The Maharasha offers an astounding clarity on how Hashem runs the world. He answers that every action you take creates a spiritual force called a Malach.
Every word you say creates a Malach.
EVERY THOUGHT creates a Malach.
Those Malachim *we create* are the forces who help us go in the direction we choose to go.

Hashem's perfect design of the physical world is matched in the spiritual world.
This means that everything we say, do and think makes a difference!
We create forces, Malachim, which bring about what we are actually attracting to ourselves. So in a single day, we create millions of forces with our thoughts, words and every action, these are creating *for us* a momentum in that direction.

If I think and talk about my **fears and worries**, I create spiritual forces which accompany me in the direction of my fears and worries!!
If I think and talk about my **stress** again and again, I am literally creating Malachim which guide me in that direction and help bring about more reasons for me to experience stress!!
If a person has an **addiction** and it occupies their thoughts, their words, their actions, he creates the forces which help bring him more and more into his addiction!

---

186 Makkos. 10b. The Gemora is explaining how Hashem gives direction to sinner who just committed manslaughter by providing road signs for him to escape to the nearest city of safety, Arei Miklat. The Gemora deduces that if Hashem is so kind to guide a Choteh to find his way to safety, how much more so for a Tzadik (or Beinoni). The point being, Hashem is always helping us go in His ways, we may not be aware of His directions if we are not looking or listening very closely. See also Avot. 4:11. - רַבִּי אֱלִיעֶזֶר בֶּן יַעֲקֹב אוֹמֵר, הָעוֹשֶׂה מִצְוָה אַחַת, קוֹנֶה לוֹ פְּרַקְלִיט אֶחָד. וְהָעוֹבֵר עֲבֵרָה אַחַת, קוֹנֶה לוֹ קַטֵּיגוֹר אֶחָד.
187 מהרש"א, הרב אליעזר הלוי אידלס שמואל המהרשא הרב. Born 1555, died 1631. One of the most outstanding commentaries on Shas Bavli, he was the leader of several communities in his life time, including Rabbi of Lublin, Chelem, Ostrog and Tiktin.

Thanks to modern 'target advertising' we can so easily understand this Chazal and the Maharasha! We see how technology can lure us to buy and buy, but it is not random advertising, they know precisely how to show us what we are most likely to buy *because we have already gone in that very direction.*
We are the ones feeding the direction we go in!

The more we think good thoughts, happy thoughts, grateful thoughts, thoughts of the many blessings in our life, the more we create Malachim to accompany us and *help us see more blessings* and *those same Malachim help us see reasons to be grateful.*[188]

The more we complain, talk about what we do not like, accuse others of wrongdoing, argue and hate, the more Malachim we create to guide us down the slippery slope of anger, resentment, complaining, and hatred! Those Malachim help us see more reasons for us to complain and experience what we do not like in our lives! We literally hold the reins of our own destiny!

So how do we break a habit of complaining that we have had for years or even decades?
How can we stop the millions of Malachim accompanying me in that same direction?

The Difficult News
I have created so many Malachim pushing me in my bad habit!
When I want to overcome my Yetser Hara (thought in the moment) for anger with my friend, parent, child, spouse, I may find it very hard.
If I do not realize how many Malachim I have created with my angry thoughts and words, I will not understand why I have such a hard time stopping my anger.
The 'Anger Forces' I created are leading me down the *anger road* and so the momentum of possibly thousands or even millions of Malachim are what I have to now overcome with a new commitment to break my anger. No wonder it is so so hard! So what can I possibly do to break the momentum behind my addictions, my anger, my craving for unhealthy foods, my leaning toward judging others unjustly so easily?

---

188 This is a deeper meaning into the words of David HaMelech, Tehilim 81:11 - הַרְחֶב־פִּיךָ וַאֲמַלְאֵהוּ - 'Widen your mouth and I will fill it.' Meaning, when you widen your mouth with more smiles of joy and gratitude for Hashem's blessings in your life, Hashem will fill your mouth with even more reasons to praise and thank Him. It is your thank yous which causes Hashem to give you even more blessings and reasons to be grateful - fill your mouth with more praise!

The Good News
Your past never equals your future! Ever!
Because Hashem created in us the power to change direction in ONE THOUGHT! Yes! Teshuva takes one thought,[189] one word (sorry). Your very next thought is where you exist! Never in yesterday's thoughts or even tomorrow's thoughts. The past is history and the future never exists because the moment you arrive in the future, it is the now! So the only real you is your immediate thought.

There are no addiction problems, only *thinking* problems!
We *think* that this food will comfort us, or we *think* this drug will take us out of our pain, etc.
The problem is not the addiction, the problem is *thinking* one needs to escape one's misery with this item he is addicted to.
The problem is not the food, the problem starts with *thinking* this food will comfort me.
It's not the traffic stressing me out, it's my *thinking* about the traffic that is stressing me out!

So the key to changing a habit is to *know* the habit is only made up of thought in the moment. Sounds simple, because it is!

The fact that I have spent thousands or millions of thoughts in the past thinking about this habit does not change my chances of changing the next thought.

The next thought is always your choice.

Even though the millions of times you thought about your habit in the past created millions of Malachim now knocking on the door of your mind to let the thoughts in, you still have total control of your next thought! That is the power of Teshuva.

---

189 Hashem created Teshuva before He began Creation of the universe because it is not part of the laws of nature, it is beyond the laws of nature. Teshuva is the very reason why Hashem declared the world is exceedingly good only minutes after Adam ate from the tree and set back the Tikun HaOlam by thousands of years. Hashem knew that Teshuva has the power to fix everything so He honestly declared that the world is very good despite Adam blowing it! See Shulchan Aruch, Even HaEzer, 38:31 where the Halacha says a woman is legally married to an evil man who conditionally marries her on condition he is a Tzadik Gamur, totally righteous. Even though he is known to all to be a Rasha Gamur, totally wicked, the marriage is valid because maybe he had a thought of Teshuva! Teshuva works to totally redefine ourselves in literally one moment. The Medrash Agadda on Gen.3:12 says that had Adam admitted his mistake with one word חטאתי, Hashem would have forgiven him for eating from the Etz HaDaas. The Medrash then says that had Chava said one word - חטאתי then Hashem would have forgiven both of them! We see that one word "sorry" can erase everything of the past!

Teshuva is your next thought. When you change the direction of your next thought away from your habitual thoughts, you start winning against the habit.

What is the best next thought you can have to divert your mind away from the habitual thinking?

Say Thank You and Please!
What to say Thank You for:
In your very next thought, say '**Thank You**' to **Hashem** for giving you your Yetzer Hara to *not* listen to!

1. Thank Hashem He his not giving up hope in you - by inviting you to ignore your Yetzer Hara.
2. "Thank you Hashem for the invitation to be silent to those who hurt me with words because now I can prove to You and myself how strong I am inside."
3. "Thank You Hashem for the bully because now I can turn to *You* instead of listening to my thoughts of fear, so the bully and my fear thoughts (Yetzer Hara) make me come closer to You."
4. "Thank You Hashem for the bully so I can get the Mitzvah of אמונה because I know everything comes from You because You love me. Now I will be stronger in my Emuna because of the bully!"
5. Thank You Hashem for the bully because now I can live the Mitzvah of being Davuk to You - ובו תדבק and another Mitzvah of בכל דרכיך דעהו, to be aware of You in every direction I go in.
6. "Thank You Hashem for bully because now I get the awesome Mitzvah of showing my love for You when I have thoughts of fear"[190]
7. "Thank You Hashem for the bully because now I get the Mitzvah of not believing any other power exists except You![191] Because my Yetzer Hara makes me turn to You to save me instead of believing anything else can help me without Your help!"
8. In your next thought, you can **ask Hashem** "Please help me ignore both the bully and the fear I have of him."
9. "Thank You Hashem for my Yetzer Hara thought because now I get the Mitzvah of the Shema Yisrael when I say You are Echud, it means You Are The Only One Force in all creation, so by thanking You for my Yetzer I am saying You sent me my Yetzer to test my

---

[190] The Mitzvah to love Hashem is found in Dev. 6:5 - וְאָהַבְתָּ אֵת ה' אֱלֹקֶיךָ בְּכָל־לְבָבְךָ which Chazal tell us in Brachos 9:5 means to love Hashem with both your Yetzer Hara thoughts and Yetzer Tov thoughts - בִּשְׁנֵי יְצָרֶיךָ, בְּיֵצֶר טוֹב וּבְיֵצֶר רָע.

[191] This is the second Mitzvah in the Aseret HaDibros - Ex.20:3 - לֹא־יִהְיֶה לְךָ אֱלֹהִים אֲחֵרִים עַל־פָּנָי. Not to believe any other powers exist except Hashem.

love for you and to say ONLY YOU are the ONE Source of everything!

Thank Hashem for giving you another chance to prove your internal metal by ignoring the habitual thinking.

What to say Please for:
When the Yetzer Hara pops-up say PLEASE HASHEM help me ignore these thoughts.
PLEASE HELP ME HASHEM to divert my thoughts to You with Tefila or by opening a Sefer and learn a few lines of Torah or
PLEASE HELP ME HASHEM get busy with a business call or a social call or return a call or pay my bills.
PLEASE HELP ME HASHEM !

Of course Hashem helps us,[192] but we are the ones who have to break the habits. If we are smart, we will know Hashem is The One Who made this system and He is cheering us on to win.[193]

---

[192] Yuma 38b, bottom of the daf.
[193] See Likutei Moharan I, Lesson #233. Hashem has great pleasure from the very struggle we have when fighting and winning our Yetzer Hara, like Kings who used to compete their animals in races and fights and would cheer their side. Hashem is cheering us (kaveyachol). R' Nachman uses this mashal for Hashem, The Real King Who cheers us on when our thoughts taunt us and we win over them by ignoring the Non-Reality Thoughts.

5.0 Sipurei Tzadikim

Next best to role modeling in person is **Stories of Tzadikim** which inspire one to emulate their actions. The number one method of 'teaching Middos' is role modeling from true Talmidei Chachamim and Tzadikim. The next best is being inspired by stories of the same. Today, there is a plethora of Judaica books on every subject of Torah, and no less on the topic of biographies of our Gedolim both today and in previous generations. The Torah life style has literally created millions of Tzadikim and Tzidkanios in the past 3,379 years since the giving of the Torah. Not to mention the Avos and Imahos and the Shivtei Ka.

We recommend the Rebbe and Morah read to the class or tell the class a short story every day of our Tzadikim and Gedolei Torah. Best would be to do so from a spectrum of different Tzadikim - Sephardi, Ashkenazi, Hassidic masters, so that children can be inspired to emulate our giants of Torah and Tzidkus and respect all factions in Klal Yisrael, no matter their specific identity.

Rabbi Nachman of Breslov attributed all his Madreigos to the inspiration he had as a child of 6 years old from the stories he heard in his home from Talmidim of the Baal Shem Tov.[194]

1. **Stories of Tzadikim**[195]
2. **Stories of Inspiration available on CD/MP3,** downloadable in the class room go **to www.torahcommunications.org**
3. **Stories of Inspiration from Rabbi Mordecai Finkleman or www.jewisheverything.net or call 323-931-8923**
4. **Imamother.com** also great resource for children's stories.
5. **Rabbi Shalom Arush's Sefer Garden of Miracles. Say "Thank You" & See Miracles. 190 true stories about the power of gratitude**
6. **Biographies of Tzadikim & Gedolim.**[196]
7. **Kids Speak series.**
8. **Books on Middos - Honorable Mentchen, etc. Child Safety**

---

[194] He himself being the great grandson of the Baal Shem Tov claimed that it was not his Neshama or Yichus that helped him become a towering Tzadik but rather his own efforts. He said this was true of all Tzadikim too and nobody is less able to become a Tzadik than anyone else since it all depends on the same on item - effort. Sichot HaRan #158, #165, #166, #170.

[195] Likutei Moharan I, Lesson 248 & 234. He explains how stories of Tzadikim can inspire a person to greatness in Torah and Tefilah and Massim Tovim, as well as purify one's thoughts.

[196] A word of caution - stories of how they were born brilliant are more likely to inject yiyush than inspiration! But the stories of their exemplary behavior Bein Adam Lechavero and avodas Hashem, tefila, simcha, hitchazkut, etc, are truly inspiring.

6.0 The Art of The Deal - *How to sell anything to anyone!*
We will now explore the simple mechanics of what makes a student want to learn from his teacher. The winning formula that makes a teacher a master teacher is not mysterious, but actually a science. Follow the simple formula and you are planning for success!

6.1 Three Parts to The Sale.
There is a powerful parallel between the world of 'sales' and 'teaching.'[197]

Here is the premise: If we know how a successful salesperson is able to *sell almost anything to anyone*, we will be on our way to understanding what makes an outstanding teacher able to win the mind and heart of his customers (students) and sell them (teach) his subject in a way that his students 'buy' whatever he sells them!

Actually, this parallel is based on the meaning of וְשִׁנַּנְתָּם לְבָנֶיךָ which will be explained at the end of the Art of the Deal. We will also reveal the answer to the question: Is the Art of The Deal about how to *convince the customer* to buy, or more about how to help the customer *convince himself* of the true value of your product?

There are three parts to the sale: The Salesperson, The Customer & The Product.

> **6.1** You, the **Teacher**, are a **Salesperson** by default!
> **6.2** Your **Student** is your **Customer**.
> **6.3** The **Torah**, its values and lifestyle are the **Products** you are selling to your customer.

We will look at each one of these:

6.1 You, the teacher are a salesperson by default!

To truly grasp the persona of a master teacher, we need to let go of the very title 'teacher' and re-look at Hashem's definition in His dictionary. In Lashon Hakodesh, the term מלמד , מורה , רבי and מחנך are popularly translated as a 'teacher.' The actual meaning of each one of these Hebrew terms reveals the true

---
[197] I heard this from Mr. Avi Shulman. He likened a teacher to a salesman and the student to his customer. The parallel is very striking when we explore what we are selling and how students 'buy' from their teachers what they learn from them.

definition of your identity as a 'teacher' and indeed, the mechanics of a master teacher.[198]

Rebi - רבי comes from the two letter root רב which means 'many,' 'abundance, 'a lot.' What does a Rebi have to have an abundance of? He needs to have a *lot* of Torah knowledge, a *lot* of patience, *abundance* of love and respect for his students, he needs to have a *lot* of Yiras Shamayim and Middos Tovos. Looking closer at this idea, would you agree a רבי also needs to recognize that he does not have a class of 20 students in front of him as much as he has 20 *different* minds in his class? In which case he needs an *abundance* of ways to reach different students! He cannot just have one way of teaching if his style does not match the needs of each student! He needs *many* tools in his bag to reach different styles of learning. On even closer look, we see the Hebrew Shoresh רב also shares the same root as ריב which means 'conflict' or 'strife.'[199] The goal of a Rebi has to be to help the student see a problem, contradiction in the text, conflict of opinions and then help the student find a solution! The Rebi has the function of drawing his students into the *conflict* or *battle* of minds which is classically called מלחמתא של תורה - 'The *battle* of Torah!'

Morah - מורה means 'Director' or 'guide' from the lashon of מורה חץ which means an 'archer' who *directs* the arrow to its target.[200] The Morah is not a 'teacher' she is one who knows how to direct the student to the target, the goal of the learning which is always independence. Whether it means directing the child to find the answer on their own (independence) or helping the child learn the shape of letters, nekudos, self-correct when they make mistake instead of being told the answer or told the correct reading of the word.

---

198 Please refer to the DVDs on Hashkafa in Chinuch where this is dealt with more fully, for the sake of clarity, we are repeating main points here.
199 See Rashi on Dev. 33:7 on the words "יָדָיו רָב לוֹ" - Rashi comments - יָדָיו רָב לוֹ. יָרִיבוּ רִיבוֹ. See also Tehilim 43:1 and Shmuel I. 25:39.
200 See Yishayahu 37:33 - וְלֹא-יוֹרֶה שָׁם חֵץ - '...don't shoot an arrow there...' So a Morah is someone who guides the student (arrow) to find the (target) answer themselves! The lashon of הוראה and יורה is one of guiding as found in Tehilim 25:12 - מִי זֶה הָאִישׁ יְרֵא ה' יוֹרֶנּוּ בְּדֶרֶךְ יִבְחָר - 'One who fears Hashem, He (G-d) will **guide** him in the way he will choose. See Tehilim 86:11 where the Yalkut Shimoni says the lashon of הוֹרֵנִי ה' דַּרְכֶּךָ means a lashon of הדרכה - guiding. See also Radak on Shmuel I, 30:31. See also Yishayahu 28:9 - יוֹרֶה דֵעָה - means 'direct (the) mind.' See Shmuel I, 31:3 - הַמּוֹרִים - 'the archers.' See also Mishley 26:18. See also Divrei Hayamim, I. 10:3.

The Morah is expert (archer) at aiming at the target, the child's specific learning style (על פי דרכו) and mind. When the Morah reaches her target, the child's way of learning, she has hit the bull's eye! Chazal reveal another aspect of a Morah, that the lashon of **הוראה** comes from the three letter root **הרה** which means 'pregnant'. Claims Yalkut Shimoni,[201] Hashem is The One Who causes a person to be re-born with the 'guidance' Hashem give them. This will be explained more in the next term - Melamed.

Melamed - A **מלמד** is someone who assists in the birth of wisdom in the mind of the student. This is the meaning as explained in Metzudas David.[202] This has huge ramifications for teachers. We are literally re-defining our identity according Hashem's dictionary of who a Melamed truly is. He is here to help the child give birth to his own wisdom! The implication is that the student has already been endowed with Divine Intelligence and innate wisdom, the job of the Melamed is to help the student draw it out from themselves. The most obvious predicate here is that we already knew the entire Torah on a Neshama level when we were in our mother's womb learning from a Malach. At our exit, we forgot it all, so all future learning Torah is actually a process of 'retrieval,' revealing what is already inside.

Knowing this meaning of **מלמד** helps us identify the greatest teacher we ever had! You will easily recall the teacher in your life who had the most influence upon you. But I refer here to *The Teacher* of all teachers. We refer to Hashem every morning in Birkas HaTorah as **המלמד** תורה לעמו ישראל. Now we can appreciate that Hashem as The Melamed is not referring to Him as our *teacher* but rather *The One Who causes birth of Torah inside us.*

---

201 Yalkut Shimoni on Shemos 4:12 - וְעַתָּה לֵךְ וְאָנֹכִי אֶהְיֶה עִם־פִּיךָ **וְהוֹרֵיתִיךָ** אֲשֶׁר תְּדַבֵּר - Hashem tells Moshe Rabeynu to go to Paroh with Aron and that He (Hashem) will be give Moshe Rabeynu the right words to say and will guide Aron's mouth to know what to say. The Yalkut writes on this - אני עושתך בריה חדשה כאשה זו שהיא **הרה** ויולדת - which means Hashem is encouraging Moshe Rabeynu about his mission to Paroh and tells him He will make Moshe Rabeynu like a new born just like a lady giving birth by **guiding** him with the right words to say. See also Shmuel I. 12:23, Metzudat there.

202 See Mishely 23:24-25 - גִּיל אֲבִי צַדִּיק וְיוֹלֵד חָכָם יִשְׂמַח בּוֹ: כֹּה יִשְׂמַח־אָבִיךָ וְאִמֶּךָ וְתָגֵל **יוֹלַדְתֶּךָ** - which loosely translates as - The father of the Tzadik will rejoice, and he will **cause** the **birth** of a wise son in whom he will enjoy. Your father and your mother will be happy, and she who **bore** you shall rejoice. Metzudas David on the words **וְיוֹלֵד** חָכָם pin points the means as המוליד את החכם, רוצה לומר המלמד ומוליד חכמה בלב התלמיד which means - 'The one who causes the birth of a wise son, meaning to say, he is the Melamed, because he causes birth of wisdom in the Lev/Mind of the student.' And in the next verse (Mishley 23:25) on the word **יוֹלַדְתֶּךָ** - the Metzudas David explains again - **המלמדתך המולידה החכמה בלבך** - The one who teaches you is the one who causes you to give birth to the wisdom in your mind!' So you see how a Melamed is a master teacher when he is NOT teaching but causing learning to be drawn from inside the student.

He is The One Who gifts us His wisdom, understanding and Daas.[203] It is His Divine Wisdom already inside us that we are giving birth to when we learn Torah. The job of the 'teacher' is to *cause his student to learn* much more than to teach him what he does not know. When a Melamed helps a child see how they were able to come to the question and answer themselves, he is fulfilling his task as a master Melamed.

A Mechanech - מחנך has six meanings in Lashon HaKodesh. When we look at them all, we will see the ingredients that make up a Master Mechanech. When translated as 'teacher' or 'educator' we are missing out on the precious Hashkafa the real word is intended to impart.

מחנך and חנוך share the same two letter root חן, which usually translates as 'grace,' charm' or 'favor.' The Torah definition of חן is a קשר שאינו נראה - 'an invisible connection.'[204] This refers to what the teacher is thinking and feeling. What a person *thinks* immediately creates his *feeling*, both thought and feeling are invisible to others till you express your thoughts in words or body language.

When the teacher has thoughts of trust in his student's innate intelligence, believes in the student's Neshama and Divinely programmed desire to learn, discover, explore, the student will invisibly connect to the teacher because כַּמַּיִם הַפָּנִים לַפָּנִים כֵּן לֵב־הָאָדָם לָאָדָם [205]- just like waters reflect the facial expressions, so too does the mind and heart of one person reflect his friend. This formula refers to any relationship, be it teacher-student or husband-wife, parent-child. We are all wired the same.

This Passuk reveals that if I truly want to influence another, focus on what I am thinking! Don't bother trying to change your spouse, start with yourself. So the word חן really means *invisible connection*. A מחנך is thus a 'connector,' someone who connects with his students.[206]

---

203 As the Anshei Kenesset HaGedola expressed in the first of the middle Berachos of Shemoneh Esrei - אַתָּה חוֹנֵן לְאָדָם דַּעַת, וּמְלַמֵּד לֶאֱנוֹשׁ **בִּינָה**. חָנֵּנוּ **מֵאִתְּךָ** דֵּעָה, בִּינָה וְהַשְׂכֵּל. בָּרוּךְ אַתָּה יְיָ, חוֹנֵן הַדָּעַת.
204 This is the exact definition I heard from Rabbi Yaakov Greenwald z"l quoting the Steipler Gaon z"l with whom he wrote the sefer Eitzos V'hadrachos.
205 Mishley 27:19. Rashi explains that as one knows his friend loves him, he too loves his friend back. Some call this 'the law of reciprocation.'
206 This was how I heard it explained by Rabbi Greenwald z"l in the name of the Steipler z"l.

The word חן throughout TaNaCh is translated by Targum[207] as רחמין which comes from the root רחם - womb. רחמין or in Hebrew רחמים is translated as 'mercy' or 'compassion.' The womb of course is the one place in the entire universe where a recipient receives everything for nothing! The growing child in the womb receives warmth, insulation, protection, nutrition and does nothing in return (except some kicking and discomfort to Mum!). It is the ultimate giving and compassion with no immediate expectation of any reciprocation. Instead, the mother is carrying her child with the total expectation to nurture this child for many more years to come till he/she is independent (usually around 36 years old! Sorry, just joking!). So now we have the second meaning in חנוך. The Mechanech is here to connect to the child and show kindness and compassion, giving the child plenty of chances to learn Torah till the student can learn on his own.

The third meaning is also related to the Targum's רחמין because this is the exact same translation for every time the word אהב - love - appears in the Torah. In other words, חן and אהבה both refer to Rachamim, compassion. The Master Mechanech is a connector - חן, and someone who gives many chances and who *loves* his students.

The fourth meaning of חנוך is 'train' and 'start again.' This is found in Gen.14:14
וַיִּשְׁמַע אַבְרָם כִּי נִשְׁבָּה אָחִיו וַיָּרֶק אֶת־חֲנִיכָיו יְלִידֵי בֵיתוֹ שְׁמֹנָה עָשָׂר וּשְׁלֹשׁ מֵאוֹת וַיִּרְדֹּף עַד־דָּן
Avraham heard the news of his nephew's capture and engaged his 'trained' men to go to battle and redeem Lot.
Rashi tells us the word חֲנִיכָיו means 'his trained men in Mitzvos[208]' - שֶׁחִנֵּךְ אוֹתָן לַמִּצְווֹת
Rashi then adds:
וְהוּא לְשׁוֹן הַתְחָלַת כְּנִיסַת הָאָדָם אוֹ כְּלִי לְאֻמָּנוּת שֶׁהוּא עָתִיד לַעֲמוֹד בָּהּ
Rashi explains חנוך as *training* to be a term that means to *start* something. For example, a person *starts* training in a craft or skill which he will eventually be able to do on his own.
One example Rashi gives to illustrate how training has a beginning and one starts again and again till one is fully trained is "וְכֵן "חֲנוֹךְ לַנַּעַר" 'train a Na'ar.'[209]

---

207 Megilla 3a tells us that the Targum was actually part of the Mesora from Sinai.
208 See Medresh Aggada on this pasuk who adds that they were trained in the Mitzvos of War. See also Rashi's rendering of the word Chinuch in Old French as אֶנְצֵינַיְי"ר - or הדריך -in Lashon HaKodesh which means 'guide' or 'direct.' Either way, they are all pointing to the function of a Mechanech being a 'trainer' and 'guide' as opposed to 'teacher.'
209 The other two examples Rashi offers show how חנוך is related to starting/initiating are חֲנֻכַּת הַמִּזְבֵּחַ 'Inauguration of the Mizbayach.' Num. 7:10. The *first time* the Mizbayach was used for

The second meaning Rashi offers is that the word Chinuch is the term adopted to describe '*initiation* or *starting*' as in חֲנֻכַּת הַמִּזְבֵּחַ and חֲנֻכַּת הַבַּיִת.

'Training' means 'starting again and again' till you are fully[210] trained.
So a מְחַנֵךְ is a 'trainer' who helps his student start again and again, repeats the lesson as many times till the student knows it by himself.

חנוך is also the language of '*tailoring*,' making something '*customized*.' We see this in the Mishna in Moed Katan[211] which talks about hewing out the stone inside a catacomb (grave inside a wall of a cave) *to the size of the corpse* - מְחַנְּכִים אֶת הַכּוּכִין. So you, as a Mechanech are a 'master tailor' who knows how to tailor the learning to the specific needs of your students. A master tailor does not force the same size clothing on every customer! Neither does the grave digger force every corpse to fit the size of the catacomb, and neither will the master teacher use one style of teaching with the mistaken assumption that 'one size fits all!'

Lastly, the word חנוך is made up of the letters - חן and כו. כו is the famous Gematria 26, of Hashem's Name YKVK. Thus, Chinuch means '*connect*' the child to *Hashem*.'

Korbanos. And "חֲנֻכַּת הַבַּיִת" 'Inauguration of the House.' Tehilim 30:1. The *beginning* of the Avodah in the Bais Hamikdash.

210 In his closing words, Rashi reveals the ultimate goal of 'training' - שֶׁהוּא עָתִיד לַעֲמוֹד בָּהּ - 'that he will train till he can stand in it.' The term '*stand*' throughout Chazal expresses *independence*. Even the expression in English '*to stand on one's own two feet*' means he is self-sufficient and independent. This is very significant because when a child first learns to stand by himself, he will have already fallen hundreds of times before he stands without falling. Each time he stood and fell, his leg muscles became a drop stronger in order to carry his upper torso. The very first Mishna in Avos demonstrates the same idea when the success of the Mesora depends on three items, including - וְהַעֲמִידוּ תַלְמִידִים הַרְבֵּה - usually translated as 'establish many students.' However, on closer examination, you will notice the rule in dikduk of Lashon Hakodesh usually places the adjective before the noun. So if you want to say 'many students' it would be 'הַרְבֵּה תַלְמִידִים.' But the Mishna places the adjective *after* the noun which suggests a different instruction from the Anshei Kenesset HaGedola, which is '*stand up students many times*.' The emphasis of הַרְבֵּה is not only a possible reference to the number of students but also to the many times the Rebbe has to help them stand up on their own. The ultimate purpose of training our students is for them to become *independent* in Torah to continue the Mesorah themselves into the next generation without you!

211 Moed Katan 1:6 - אֵין חוֹפְרִין כּוּכִין וּקְבָרוֹת בַּמּוֹעֵד, אֲבָל מְחַנְּכִים אֶת הַכּוּכִין בַּמּוֹעֵד

In summary:
- The master מחנך knows how to '*connect*' to children, he finds חן in their eyes through his own thoughts and feelings about them.
- He loves his students and has compassion for them (like a nurturing womb).
- He will give his students as *many ways and chances* as needed till they get it right.
- He will *train* his students by *starting* again and again, till they are able to do the task on their own.
- He will *tailor* the learning to the student's individual needs.

Tall order! But all these ingredients are part of the make up of the Master Mechanech. At least we now know what we are aiming to become!

6.2 Know your Customer (student)!

The second part of the Art of The Deal is the salesperson (teacher) has to know his customer. When the salesperson pays attention to the needs of the customer, he can more easily help the customer with the specific product or service that fits the needs of the customer. When the customer senses the salesperson taking a sincere interest in his needs, the customer builds trust in the salesperson. The more a teacher makes an effort to understand his students' strengths, weaknesses, talents, character, the more the teacher can tailor the Chinuch for that student. The more the student believes and trusts in his teacher.

6.3 Know the Products and services you are selling to your customer.

In our metaphor, the salesperson is the teacher who is hired to sell Torah to his customers. Let us understand the fullest extent of the products, goods and services the *teacher* is *selling* to his customers. We all know the most effective teacher/parent/adult in any child's life is the one who cares the most about that child and who role models a Torah character. So in effect, you are selling:

- A Relationship with Hashem.
- Ahavas Hashem.
- Yiras Hashem.
- Simchas HaChayim.
- Torat Emet – How we know the Torah is Emet.
- Clarity of values - Real Power.
- Mitzvot (teaching the Mitzvot and *how* to live them)

- A Meaningful life.
- Values.
- Direction.
- Identity - Part of an international community of Torah Jews (in an unbroken Mesora!).
- Self-Esteem.
- Self-Confidence.
- Self-Respect.
- Respect for others.
- Love for others.
- Love for life.
- Work ethic.
- Academically you are selling:
- Specific skills.
- Aleph Bais recognition.
- Nekudos recognition.
- Blending.
- Reading Accuracy
- Reading Fluency.
- Sherashim, vocabulary.
- Prefixes.
- Suffixes.
- Basic Dikduk.
- Textual skills in Chumash/Nach.
- Textual skills in Mishna
- Textual skills in Gemora.
- Etc.

A student (customer) who realizes how much value you are teaching them and enabling them to discover in themselves, such a student will be your student for life. If you are role modeling this list above, your student will attribute you as his single biggest influence.

6.5 The Art of The Sale:

There is no mystery to the secret of successful salespeople, it's a scientific formula. Mess with the formula, lose the customer!

Three Parts to the Sale:
1. Rapport   +
2. Value   +
3. Relevance = Sold

1. Define Rapport:
When a teacher has built rapport with his student (ingredients of the 'rapport recipe' listed below) you are building deep trust in the child for you. It is this type of rapport that opens the mind and heart of the student to learn from you (repeat customer).

- Sincerity[212] (sincere interest in fulfilling the needs of your customer)
- Respect[213]
- Honesty
- Trust
- Confidence
- Track record of success – millions of Yidden have lived righteous lives for thousands of years!
- Love, appreciation, gratitude.

2. Define Value & Relevance
- Teaching skills
- Self-confidence
- Self-esteem
- Love for learning
- Experience myself maturing
- My teacher helps me reveal my own innate health/resilience
- My teacher role models for us the Mitzvah of Tochacha so we can learn how to resolve conflict ourselves.
- My teacher gives so many ways for us to remember how we are always strong and never defeated.
- My teacher gives us direction on the bullying
- I am not afraid of being wrong

---

212 Avot 2:8,9. Lev Tov wins hands down against all other desirable Middos. Lev Tov usually translates as a good heart, but that is only because one has a good mind or good thoughts.

213 Avot 4:12 - רַבִּי אֱלְעָזָר בֶּן שַׁמּוּעַ אוֹמֵר, יְהִי כְבוֹד תַּלְמִידְךָ חָבִיב עָלֶיךָ כְּשֶׁלָּךְ. See Berachos 28b, when the students of Rebi Eliezer Ben Hurkuness asked on his death bed for advice that would earn them life in both this and the next world, he responded - "be clear and thus careful with the respect due to your peers!" - תנו רבנן: כשחלה רבי אליעזר, נכנסו תלמידיו לבקרו. אמרו לו: רבינו, למדנו אורחות חיים **הזהרו בכבוד חבריכם**. אמר להם: ונזכה בהן לחיי העולם הבא. The word **הזהרו** comes from the three letter root **זהר** which means 'light' or 'shine' or 'clarity.' It is also the same root as **זהירות** which usually translates as 'being careful.' The connection between 'clarity' and 'careful' is simply the more one is 'clear' about the true value of another person's kavod, dignity, the more 'careful' one will be in how he treats others.

- My teacher has created an emotionally safe classroom
- My teacher has expanded my vocabulary exponentially so that my natural curiosity leads me to be a ferocious reader.
- My teacher has expanded my vocabulary so that I can read books which open my mind Hashem's beautiful world.
- My teacher constantly connects what we are learning to the History time line so that I constantly strengthen my understanding of why I live the way I do, why I believe in the Torah and the millions of Tzadikim over the past 3,000 years!

3. Define Sold

At this point, your customer will pay almost any price to buy from you because he sees the value of what you are teaching (selling) as greater than any price he is willing to pay.

וְשִׁנַּנְתָּם לְבָנֶיךָ is the Torah source[214] for 'teaching' Torah to our students. However, the actual word שִׁנּוּן does not mean teach, it has five meanings, all correlate to give us the ingredients of the master 'teacher' who can sell Torah to his students. שִׁנּוּן means '*repeat*' and also '*sharpen.*' In its two letter root it means tooth from the word שֵׁן which does the primary act of '*chewing.*' So what does it mean to 'teeth' and 'chew' to your children? The only time children really see your teeth is when you are smiling! The only time a child really knows that you love what you are eating is in the moment where he sees you savor the taste while you are 'chewing' the food! In other words, the Torah is giving us a full service description of the master teacher. The master teacher smiles and is excited about Torah, Mitzvos and a relationship with Hashem. Those are the core values a teacher imparts to his students. The method of delivery has to be prefaced with the child connecting to the teacher. The teacher's smile does exactly that. שִׁנּוּן also means *repeat* and *sharpen* because mastery of Torah comes after many reviews and the mastery that comes from review is what prepares the student to be able to drill down, because now he has more information to compare and contrast. So review is preparation for Iyun.

You are a member of a nation of successful salespeople. A member of the most successful nation in world history who have a track record of successfully selling the same product and services to the next generation of customers. Your nation's successful Mesora of the same Torah, Mitzvos and values is so impressive because you have

---

214 Dev. 6:7.

done so while being the most despised, hated, persecuted, expelled and people in world history. The secret of your success is the fact that you have Hashem, The Ultimate Melamed, Teacher Who guaranteed His Torah would never be forgotten![215] So you are a team member of the winning team and you not only have the great reward awaiting you for your efforts in helping the next generation of children continue the Mesora till Mashiach,[216] you also have the merit of justifying all the efforts of every teacher who came before you who invested in the next generation. Ashreichem V'Ashrei Chelkeichem! In the immeasurable merit of your choice to give to the next generation of pure Jewish Neshamos, may Hashem bless you with only Nachas from all your children till Mashiach's arrival, may it be soon in our days, Amen V'Amen!

---

215 Dev. 31:21 - וְהָיָה כִּי־תִמְצֶאןָ אֹתוֹ רָעוֹת רַבּוֹת וְצָרוֹת וְעָנְתָה הַשִּׁירָה הַזֹּאת לְפָנָיו לְעֵד **כִּי לֹא תִשָּׁכַח מִפִּי זַרְעוֹ**.
See also Yeshayahu 59:20-21 - וַאֲנִי זֹאת בְּרִיתִי אוֹתָם אָמַר ה' רוּחִי אֲשֶׁר עָלֶיךָ וּדְבָרַי אֲשֶׁר־שַׂמְתִּי בְּפִיךָ לֹא־יָמוּשׁוּ מִפִּיךָ וּמִפִּי זַרְעֲךָ וּמִפִּי זֶרַע זַרְעֲךָ אָמַר ה' מֵעַתָּה וְעַד־עוֹלָם

216 See Sefer Madraigat HaAdam, Chelek Mezakeh HaRabim, by Rabbi Yosef Hurwitz of Navardok.

Made in the USA
Coppell, TX
10 March 2024